SHOW YOUR WORK

SUCCESSFUL WOMEN SHARE THE BUMPY ROADS TO THEIR BIGGEST WINS

ANDREA ROSS   KRISTI KOETER

DIANA MALDONADO   CHRISTY JAYNES   MEG HAYS

NATASHA ZIKE   BETSY R. DAVIS   CAROL MEYER

MEGAN MANN   SANDY STEWART   JANENE NIBLOCK

SYLVIA WORSHAM   STACY JOHNSON

SULIT
PRESS

CONTENTS

Ready to fast track your publishing career, increase your visibility, or boost your business?

Harness the power of partnership by contributing a 3,000-word chapter to one of our upcoming Multi-Author Books!

If you are…

☑ Inspired by what you do and want to generously share what you've learned…
☑ Committed to meeting deadlines and doing your best work…
☑ Ready to connect with other aspiring authors who are as excited as you are to share your book with the world…

Then our Multi-Author Book might be the right path for you!

Learn more at sulitpress.com/multi-author-books

INTRODUCTION

Unless I missed it, there's no fail-proof, ten-step blueprint you can follow to map your way to success. Perhaps this is because each of us has our own definition of success, and even if you could carefully plot your way from here to there, you might not necessarily like the destination…or the journey. No roadmap or crystal ball could ever replace the painful, exhilarating, challenging, and ultimately satisfying process of navigating the bumpy road to your biggest wins.

For us women, the road to success is often as much about facing our own self-doubts as it is about taking risks. Before we even get the courage to make the pitch, pursue the degree, or chase the dream, we do battle with our own demons. *Are we even worthy of success? What if we don't measure up—to ourselves and those around us?* We've come to believe that if one thread comes loose, our whole lives could unravel. And sometimes they do. And yet we try to maintain the façade that we have it all together.

So when we scroll through social media and see someone else's "mountain top" moment, we rarely see the struggle that went along with it. Few successful women snap pics of their sleepless nights, the burned dinners, the rejections, and the pitches that weren't perfect.

They don't talk about the pain of continuing the business when their business partner no longer wants to be their spouse—or be faithful. They don't talk about showing up to an interview and being told before it even begins that they won't get the job just because they're a woman.

The trouble with maintaining a flawless façade is it forces us to figure everything out by ourselves, which can be lonely, exhausting, and extremely inefficient.

The goal is not to be perfect; the goal is to fail forward, pick yourself up when you fall, recalibrate your approach, and try again until you get a better outcome.

There are, however, a few rare, safe spaces where women can show up simultaneously as both accomplished professionals *and* works-in-progress. This book is one of those spaces. You are about to read stories from thirteen authors who have generously shared their heartfelt, honest (sometimes brutally honest) stories that will grab you by the lapels and pull you in close. Through their tears and triumphs and gathered wisdom, you'll gain the tools and inspiration you need to navigate the bumps between you and your next big win.

It's time to let down your hair, evolve along with your goals, and involve others in the process. While your definition of success is uniquely your own, you don't have to do it perfectly or get there alone. From messy middles to mountain-top moments, it's time to *Show Your Work*!

Michelle Savage

Founder, Sulit Press

www.sulitpress.com

1

LEGACY

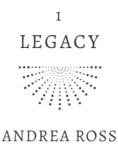

ANDREA ROSS

"Twenty-one times!" I stutter into the phone.

"What?" my sister's groggy voice comes back. Despite now only being three hours behind her, I still tend to call past her bedtime.

"Twenty-one times," I say louder!

"What twenty-one times?"

"Meals," I clarify, my voice shaking, "I have to feed them twenty-one times A WEEK!"

There's a pause, and I hear rustling noises as I assume she gets up and leaves her husband to enjoy his sleep in peace.

She comes back on, and her voice is louder but still calm. She has been a rock through all this, and my appreciation almost breaks through my panic.

"I have to feed them twenty-one times a week, Caroline! I can't do it," I state.

I've been here in our double-wide for a little over two weeks. The 300 pounds of luggage we brought back with us from Cambodia is unpacked and put away, the kids are registered for school, snow falls outside my window, and I realize spring skiing is our new reality. But the only reality I can face tonight is the insurmountable cooking requirements staring down the barrel of my new life.

"Listen," my sister's matter-of-fact voice breaks me out of my reverie. "You knew this would be a change. You can do it. There's always takeout!"

Not yet ready to be jockeyed out of my pit of eternal despair, I lament the health of takeout, the laziness of it, the expense of it...

"Oh, stop," she replies, "Ask for help, go over to friends, go out to eat, you'll be fine. They don't care what they eat. They just can't be hungry."

I didn't know it that spring night, but that conversation was my first step in articulating my biggest adult-life lesson. It was when I stepped back, with the help of my sister, to see that it didn't matter that each meal was home-cooked, or perfect, or even barely edible, but that twenty-one times a week, I would figure it out, and I would never let the kids be hungry. Today might not be perfect, but I was in it for the long game—I was in it for the legacy. Sitting in that double-wide with my two kids asleep down the hall, the word legacy hadn't yet come to define what mattered, but I was starting to look up and see the big picture. As a controlling perfectionist, it was hard to not live in the moment...managing, organizing, and making it perfect, but when you're a single mom running a large tourism company, the moment could crush you. To survive, you had to look further down the road and think where you wanted to go, where you wanted your kids and business to go, how you wanted the kids to feel about their childhood, not that one meal you didn't cook tonight, but the experience of being a child of mine. I couldn't worry about every detail of my client's experience; I had a trained team to do that. I needed to focus on how they felt on the plane ride home and the emotion the trip had manifested. What was the legacy of my motherhood? What was the legacy of my CEOhood?

My long game had changed intrinsically six years before this conversation. The irony that I write this chapter on Valentine's Day is not lost on me—Valentine's Day 2006, or more specifically the day after, was, quite literally, a game changer.

I was living in Cambodia, dubbed the Kingdom of Wonder by its less-than-imaginative tourism board. My husband and I ran a boutique hotel that we had just expanded to include a spa, a pool, and family suites. The family suites had been prompted by the arrival of our little girl seven months before, feeling that if we could raise children in Cambodia, our travelers could certainly bring their children to visit the country. And travelers were our business. Journeys Within was our Southeast Asia tourism company we had founded four years earlier. Offering custom, boutique tours to Thailand, Laos, Vietnam, Myanmar, and Cambodia, Journeys Within was growing into the premier boutique travel company in the region. The same year as having Callie, we also founded Journeys Within Our Community, a 501(c)(3) working within our local communities on clean water, microfinance, and education opportunities.

It's easy to remember the time prior to Valentine's Day 2006 through rose-tinted glasses...that when it rained, we would joke "pling tri" (it's raining fish) as, magically, puddles would fill with rainwater and tiny unexplained fish. My husband had landscaped an oasis for our hotel, we ate mango and crepes and coconut curry prepared by our chef, and my nanny loved my baby as if she were her own. I was free to work and build my business while those much more talented at the task took care of the meals, the cleaning, and the baby. It was having drinks on the back porch with guests on humid evenings, it was motorcycle rides into the village to take surveys and grow our non-profit impact. It was traveling and training and growing the business with a pride I'd never felt before. But when I'm being honest with myself—when I'm being retrospective and introspective and with the understanding that time gives—it was also endless work hours, high-level stress, and a challenged marriage.

That marriage had felt less challenged the night before. We had gone out with our team to celebrate Valentine's Day and even participated in the "who knows their partner best" contest the restaurant hosted. In my memory, we won, having been together since we were nineteen, it would make sense, but maybe it was a trick of memory to make the realities of the next day starker.

I read a text—that was it. That was the simple act that changed it all. It was from his friend Sina, and his phone was sitting right next to me. Looking back, I can't help but see my act of reading it as an act of distrust, but I have to remember that was the start of the distrust, it didn't exist prior. My first thought was that he was gay! Sina was a man, after all, and the text was amorous. It took a minute for the truth to sink in, for the betrayal to sink in…that he had put a girl in his phone using Sina's name, and he was having an affair.

I don't remember the next few days. I don't know when I talked to him. I don't know when I told him I knew. I have snatches of memory…working at my desk building itineraries with tears pouring down my cheeks, laying on the floor of the shower unable to get up, and finally sitting in my office hearing him say this wasn't a one-night stand, a one-week stand, a one-month stand, but that he loved her.

It was within those moments and revelations and tears that I made the choice. The same choice I would make when later faced with twenty-one meals a week…that I was not going to curl up in a ball and be done, but instead, I would keep my eye on the prize and keep moving forward. I wouldn't let everything I had worked for and loved be ruined.

The day after my husband told me he was in love with someone else, I welcomed guests to my hotel, built custom itineraries, breastfed my daughter, and led an art class at JWOC. I wiped away the tears and invested in my legacy.

4

Fate, however, loves to play games. That fateful Valentine's Day, one night before it all changed, Couper was created. I'll never be more grateful for anything than the fact that I saw the text the next day! So, there I was, with a seven-month-old, another baby on the way, and a husband who shared the reality that he didn't feel parenting was a good fit for him. Over the next six years, we tried to find a solution. I spent more time back in the United States. I justified the extended time there as my need to open a sales and marketing office, but really it was to give me time to try to come to grips with my new reality and decide how to move forward. When I was back in Cambodia, he worked with me at the hotel every day—we were best friends and business partners—and I cried every night when he drove away. Finally, he decided he would make it work, and there were a few years of calm, of forgiveness, of emerging from the tunnel into the light, but it wasn't meant to be. At the time, I felt that love lost, but maybe with an eye on legacy, love won.

YOU'RE NOT AS IMPORTANT AS YOU THINK YOU ARE

"Mommy," Callie asks, "Srey Nut says Daddy has a girlfriend?"

Six years after that fateful Valentine's, this is where we had ended: living together but in separate rooms, raising two kids, with him leaving to see his girlfriend and me staying at home working, raising the kids, and crying in the shower. I felt that if I left, my kids would pay the price, my company would pay the price, and my family would pay the price, so I stayed.

But this—this question—it had a price tag I hadn't calculated.

I sat down with my husband and explained I couldn't do it anymore. I begged him to put the kids first, to put me first. To put us first. He couldn't.

I realized my legacy was that I gave it my all, but when it became clear I would never get what I deserved, and my children would see that lesson play out in front of them, we left. His legacy is…that he let us.

5

And that was how we got here! In a double-wide in Truckee, California, trying to figure out how to make twenty-one meals a week happen and realizing I would have to shovel the snow off the driveway in the morning.

My move from Cambodia was fraught with challenges, but one of my biggest takeaways, and a lesson I still use with my advising clients, came from a friend who didn't pull punches. I was up, working, at two in the morning, explaining to him, my houseguest, that I had to be or my team in Southeast Asia wouldn't know what to do!

"You're never as important as you think you are," he expounded from the couch.

It took me a few months to realize he was right and a few more months to accept it, but once I did, my business flourished.

Before I realized I was leaving Cambodia, I had hired an operations manager, Anna. I knew I was trying to do too much…I had offices in Thailand, Laos, Vietnam, and my head office in Cambodia. I had opened a sales and marketing office in the US that was being run by April Cole. It's funny to think back now and realize I hired her as an administrative assistant; today, she runs Kaanect, a travel coaching and Southeast Asia specialist company that helps people conceive, plan, and enjoy trips around the world. April was also instrumental in providing some of those twenty-one meals while also making them a blast! But back then, I'd only let her do so much…knowing she couldn't possibly do it better than me! I had the same approach with Anna. She could assist me, and under my brilliance, she could support the business. And then I made the choice to leave! And it became clear that managing the operations side of the business from thousands of miles away, while also raising two kids full-time, might not be possible, even with my willingness to give up sleep! So I had to hand it over. I held tight to those words…I wasn't as important as I thought I was. And guess what? She took over, and she was better at it than me!

That's right. She wrote processes and procedures and created SOPs. She managed each office, taking advantage of the strengths and weaknesses of team members. She traveled to train our guides, and our reviews got even better, our travelers were even happier, and our teams became that much more productive. It was an important lesson for me—that by being the bottleneck, I had stifled the company's growth, and it wasn't until I was forced to step back that I saw the potential of the team I had been micromanaging. That's not to say everything was perfect, it was travel, after all, but there was growth and improvement, and for once, I wasn't driving it or holding it back.

FIND YOUR MISFITS

"Think where man's glory most begins and ends, and say my glory was I had such friends."

—William Butler Yeats

I used this quote in my personal square in my senior yearbook; I fancied myself rather profound at the age of eighteen. But it also held true—I am not the type of person who has acquaintances; I have my people. It started when I was four and attending school in London. Carrie Anne, my best friend in the world, let me borrow her shoes. We are still friends today, and she would still lend me her shoes if she didn't have tiny, perfect feet that are nowhere close to my bunioned horrors! Then there were Jenny Taylor and Rebecca Johnson, who put up with me through my narcissistic and self-involved teenage years and somehow allowed me to be *me*, even when *me* wasn't all that great. My high school friends were the ones who inspired my profound yearbook quote. One of them, Ellie, is the best mom I've ever met and one of the funniest people I know. She came to the double-wide, reorganized the kitchen, and taught me to make chocolate chip pancakes, which would often count as one of the twenty-one! I shared a name and a love of adventure with my friend Andrea. She will always understand my need to do something different!

Living in Cambodia had been hard on friendships; living through infidelity and the secrets I had guarded was even harder. My move back allowed me to connect with them again, to share what had happened, and to ask for help. Ellie met me at the airport when we landed. She brought a minivan full of kids and still had space for luggage!

"Don't worry," I remember her telling me, "You can go to the bathroom and cry when we get to the house."

I remember looking at her, and for the first time in years, not feeling the need to cry. "You know what's cool?" I whispered conspiratorially back to her, "I just realized that today, for the first time in a long time, I'm not being cheated on."

I would experience the heaviness of freedom as I built my new life, but that day, I celebrated the lightness of it!

It was these "old" friends that gave me the confidence to find and build the friendships I needed to weather the single motherhood storm. The friends I met and gravitated towards were, like me, living under the heaviness and lightness of freedom. I can't remember who coined the term Misfit Moms, but it summed us up perfectly. I don't know how we all found each other, but I'm sure if I think hard, I can remember how each of them came into my life...a gymnastics class here, a ski buddy there, but with our kids as our common language, we found each other. Lisa, who despite losing her husband in a plane crash, managed to work full-time, keep it all together, and make us all laugh. Anne, who had lost her husband to drugs (he was alive but also lost), was always willing to feed us, care for us, and watch a kid or two. Amy, dealing with a husband and joint custody, had a daughter Callie's age and an always-open bottle of wine, leading to chats and laughter. April had a husband, who was not lost, but we let her be a Misfit because she completed us; to be fair, she completed me. Sometimes, some of our greatest loves are brilliant redheads who never stop believing in us. We all became each other's support system. Need someone to watch your kids? No problem. Need one of those twenty-one meals? Ask Anne! Need help moving? They were there. I would not have survived those years without the Misfit Moms. We were sister wives...without the irritating husband.

As a business owner, your support system becomes that much more important. I was still working and traveling all the time, but with my parents living nearby, and the Misfits willing to step in any time I needed help, I was able to put time and energy into growing the business. And grow it we did. April and I built an amazing team in the US, and Anna, the now indispensable operations manager, built an amazing team in Southeast Asia.

Now, as a business advisor, I often look for my clients' misfits. Sometimes I'll even ask them, "Who is supporting you? Who are you bouncing ideas off of? Who is making dinner when you're busy?" For some of my clients, minus the dinners, I fill this role for them, and I take it with the utmost responsibility because if I hadn't had the support of my team and my friends, I would not have had the success I did. Find your support network, build your team, and surround yourself with people who support you, believe in you, and bring you joy!

MY LEGACY

It was through another friend, an honorary Misfit Mom, that the articulation of legacy really took flight. The idea of legacy has been with me forever...in my desire to give my children a life less ordinary, in my future vision of what I wanted my company to achieve and the impact I wanted it to have on our local communities, and in my ability to see what I was aiming for, well beyond the daily moments and mistakes. I hadn't yet articulated this and allowed it to become my rallying cry until Karen. It was the conversations I had with Karen and trying to show her that we could step out of the moment and into the long game that helped me articulate my own legacy. Karen was my personal trainer, and she was magical. We talked about everything. She became more of a life coach than a trainer—she built both my physical and emotional strength. It was in one of our deep conversations (probably while I was still desperately trying to do a single pull-up) that I turned to her and said, "Well, you know, it's not about today. It's about the legacy." And there it was. So simple when spoken aloud. So empowering to stop thinking about every mistake we make with our kids, with our businesses, with our personal choices, and instead to think: five, ten, twenty years from now, what will still be standing, still be felt, still be happening because of me.

So, I sit here now, Valentine's Day 2023, and think of my legacy. My company was acquired five years ago, but it still lives on, an amazing part of Wild Frontiers, a UK-based company that does valuable community work around the world on top of the unique trips they offer. My offices in Southeast Asia are now owned by the teams that Anna and I developed, trained, and believed in, and they're running them successfully and creating trips of a lifetime! That is my legacy!

Journeys Within Our Community continues to run in Cambodia—thousands of people have access to clean water, affordable microloans, and in its latest iteration, scholarships and educational opportunities. The ripple effects are infinite. That is my legacy!

April now runs Kaanect. She is a complete powerhouse. I could not have done any of it without her. That is my legacy!

The Misfit Moms are heading to Mexico next month to enjoy some sun and relaxation together. We don't see each other as much as we would like, but I know I could call any of them at any time of the day, and they would ask where not why! That is my legacy!

My kid's dad lives twenty minutes away now with his wife and two children. He has a relationship with my kids that is only possible because I let go of the anger, never demonized him, and spoke the truth with kindness. I am friends with his wife, and his kids call me Aunty Drea. Love won. That is my legacy!

Callie and Couper are in the college-planning process. I read Callie's essays about overcoming weaknesses and understanding challenges. They are funny and kind and brave and smart and self-centered and worldly and broken and complete. Who they will become and the journey they will take to get there—that is my legacy!

Then there's me—by no means perfect, but the matriarch of an amazing blended family. After selling my company, I could step back and focus on what I needed and wanted. Turns out, it was a guy named Dalton. He is a good and kind person who has faced his own challenges and still chooses to do the right thing, even when it's hard. He has built his own legacy, and I'm honored to be loved by him. We laugh all the time. He brought four kids into the mix, so together, we raise six kids that belong to various people, but they're all ours; they're all part of our legacy. And yes, the irony of the fact that I now have to worry about weekly meals for a family of eight is not lost on me, but love won. That is my legacy!

And now, I advise people as they build their own legacy. I work for Cultivate Advisors, an amazing company that advises and supports small business owners. Every day I do what I love with an incredible and dynamic team. My clients are entrepreneurs and business owners who, like me, are bumping down the road to success. I get to hold their hands as they build their legacy. I get to be one of their Misfits. I talk to them about finding harmony between work and family, that you're never as important as you think you are, and that you need to surround yourself with people who believe in you and support you and make you laugh. We also talk about their financials, marketing, sales, recruiting, leadership, and productivity, but in the end, all of those things are being worked on and grown to build the legacy of the company and the company owner.

To this day, I have probably never made twenty-one meals in one week...I've slowly become a better cook, but I've also ordered delivery, microwaved, showed up uninvited to friends' houses, and eaten takeout, but we never went hungry. I let go of perfect and embraced the journey. That is my legacy!

ANDREA ROSS

Andrea founded the award-winning Southeast Asian tourism company Journeys Within, which grew into a multi-million dollar business and won numerous accolades, including a World Savers award for its community-based initiatives. She also founded Journeys Within Boutique Hotel and Journeys Within Our Community, a nonprofit 501(c)(3) based in Cambodia. In 2018, Journeys Within was acquired by Wild Frontiers, and Andrea was kept on to develop their US operations. Today, Andrea works for Cultivate Advisors as a business advisor with clients around the world looking to professionalize and scale their businesses. She loves to work on both the quantitative aspects of a business—from dissecting the financials to creating a sales strategy to developing a recruiting plan—and the qualitative side of being a business owner and navigating who they want to be as leaders. She helps business owners define their own personal and professional legacy.

https://www.andrearossadvising.com/
https://www.facebook.com/andrea.ross.1694
https://www.instagram.com/kidsfordaze/

2
LETTING GO, NOT GIVING UP

KRISTI KOETER

I've never been one for games, even as a child. My parents loved them, card games especially, and once a week, for most of my childhood, they hosted a poker night with friends. The adults sat around our worn kitchen table that was a hair too large for the cramped dining space. They took turns dealing cards and cracking jokes between moments of dead quiet when things got serious. For a time, they even played on a poker table my dad had built in our sawdust-covered garage, surrounded by shelves and shelves that held my father's tools and other found objects he would resell from his "junking adventures."

My parents didn't want to play with me so much as they wanted to teach me how to play. My father viewed this as an important life skill —a way to make extra money. He used the extra cash from poker and junking to supplement his meager means as a grocery store butcher. He was the king of side hustles before his methods had a name. Later, the game would be golf.

Unlike my dad, I wanted more than a quick buck. I was determined to do everything I could to set myself up for success later in life. I wanted a meaningful career that would pay the bills, so I wouldn't have to live paycheck to paycheck or rely on anyone for my financial needs, especially not a man. Most of my time was spent reading and writing and plotting my next move on loose-leaf paper or spiral-bound notebooks; it didn't matter what I used. What mattered was that I devised a way out of that place. If I played my cards right and studied hard, I could be a success one day.

But it's hard to be a success when deep inside you don't feel you're good enough or that you deserve love, and I didn't for a long time. A lot of those feelings came from my tough childhood, where I endured years of verbal abuse and more. I learned not that my feelings don't matter, but that I shouldn't even have them at all. So, I formed a tough outer shell. Nothing got in. Nothing got out. When I visualize that little girl, I picture a hollowed-out walnut with me cowering inside it.

One day in sixth grade, I slipped out of art class at the end of first period and called my mother from the school pay phone. I was stifling tears. I'm sure she was alarmed—what could I be calling about from school unless it was an emergency? I was distraught and didn't know what to do. Shame and disappointment burned up my cheeks.

"I, uh—I," I stammered, trying to reign in my emotions—"I got a B on my report card." As I spoke the words aloud, I lost control of myself, and the tears started flowing. It was my first B. It might as well have been the end of the world. The bell rang, and there I was, lost and alone, holding onto the phone as kids scrambled past to their next class.

I don't know what my mother said to me that day on the phone. It didn't matter because getting good grades was part of my plan, not hers. I had called to admit my failings. My perfect record was ruined. My future plans to be the first one in my family to go to college and then onto a professional career were now in question. *What was I going to do now? How would I get a scholarship? How would I pay for college?* My parents barely made ends meet—they sure couldn't do it.

I admit I can be a little doomsday-ish.

Somehow that one B wasn't the end of me. Once I recovered, I continued making plans for myself. My love of English, reading, writing, and grammar led me to the school newspaper, and that's what I did in middle school, high school, and college, too.

I became the first person in my family to attend and graduate from college, the University of Texas at Austin, one of the nation's top journalism schools. I spent fifteen years in journalism, a dozen of them at the *Austin American-Statesman*. I started as a copy editor and worked my way up to editor of the paper's websites, where I oversaw a team of people who covered breaking news and other major events. For most of my years as editor of Statesman.com, we won the Texas Associated Press Managing Editors' highest honor for best online newspaper.

When the revenues were declining and newsrooms were being gutted, I left journalism. Content marketing was taking off. I decided to see how my skills would translate in the real world. Ten years later, I had built a second successful career with a passion for brand building, storytelling, SEO, and digital marketing, primarily at an online family travel company specializing in theme parks. Yes, I earned accolades (and took a lot of trips to Disney and Universal), but I got the most joy from helping people. When I first joined, our discounted tickets were a little-known, money-saving hack used by Disney insiders. By the time I left, I would run into people in the theme parks who had not only heard of the company but had used our content—my content—to plan their trips.

Throughout my life, people have told me I am the strongest person they know. And I am strong. Super strong, super fit, super driven, super focused. And super flawed.

The truth is, I put up walls so that no one would ever realize how weak I felt. And one of my deepest insecurities was my body. I was a bigger kid, or so I thought. Looking back now, I see that my frame, something I could not change through diet or exercise, was broader than most. That didn't keep me from trying.

For years, I used athletic achievement to prove my worth and control the size of my body. And I'm sure it's tied up in my childhood, as most things are. I was the "smart one," and my sister, fifteen months younger, was the "athletic one." At first, that didn't matter because my father was obsessed with golf and wanted to make sure at least one of us landed on tour. Not being the athlete, I had other plans. Still, he made us practice every night. We'd take a shag bag up to the high school, hit all the balls, then collect them and start again. He was not a patient instructor and had a temper that could only simmer for so long as he watched us make mistake after mistake, even with his repeated instruction. "*Looky* here," he'd say in his country boy twang to ensure we were paying attention.

To help with our putting and chipping, he built a green in the backyard, complete with a sand trap, and we were forced to compete against each other after dinner to see who had to do the dishes. Soon after, we began playing in tournaments. By the time I got to high school, even though I was on the school team, I was no longer my father's focus. My sister was a genuine talent, and he put all of his attention on her.

Though I didn't think of myself as an athlete, my need to be smaller pushed me to exercise. I gravitated toward competition. *Why do anything just for fun?* I ran my first marathon in college. Later, I took up CrossFit, which pushed dieting like a drug dealer and turned every workout into a competition. And then there was Olympic lifting, which I competed in recreationally until last year. I loved that the lifts required strength and technical precision—like a golf swing. Ironically, Olympic lifting is the only one of those sports where you don't have to be lean to excel. Yet, I still used it to control my body by competing at a weight class below my actual weight, so I was always cutting.

18

Like with my feelings, I tried stuffing down my weight and insecurities as long as possible, but you can only stuff things down for so long.

~

In July 2022, I quit my job. For the first time in my life, I had no clue what I'd be doing next. It felt like jumping without a parachute. It felt like it might be a career-ending kind of quitting. I didn't want to stay, but I felt guilty for leaving. And deeply ashamed for failing.

Without a job, I figured one of two things would happen. One, I would find the uncertainty of not having a plan and having to rely on another person for my—and my children's—financial needs for the first time in my life so unbearable that I would take the first opportunity that came along. Two, I would completely lean into that uncertainty and discover who I was meant to be.

My brand-new husband made me promise I wouldn't do number one.

Less than two weeks after quitting, I decided to stop dieting.

While these two events are seemingly unrelated, if I had not quit my job, it's unlikely I would have stopped dieting, worked on healing my family and myself, and gotten the courage to start a new career—the one I had always dreamed of but had been too afraid to pursue.

When I quit, by all appearances, I had everything going for me. I was newly married to the love of my life, a successful tech exec. We had had a bumpy start, but we were starting to blend our families (his two and my three). We had moved into a light-filled Mediterranean-modern home that sat at the top of a master-planned community on the outskirts of Austin. After we put in a pool and hot tub, it was pretty close to perfect. In the three years I had known my husband, we had traveled more than I had in my entire life, visiting scenic destinations we could explore on bike or foot. For the first time in my life, I didn't have to be the breadwinner.

I could afford to quit my job, and I'd be lying if I said that wasn't an enormous factor in my decision.

By outside appearances, my job had been going well. I was recruited by the CEO of a remote startup helping teachers pass their certification exams. Four months in, I was promoted and tasked with leading the marketing team—and most of the company—in a new initiative to drive growth. It was exciting to build my own team and be part of a leadership team that was so supportive.

But we all know appearances can be deceiving. I got the promotion after my boss had been fired. I started the role just as the CEO set an ambitious goal to reverse a massive decline in customer acquisition—a goal that wasn't remotely achievable. Our shrinking customer base had more to do with outside market factors than with us. But I thought that by focusing our efforts on this one goal, we would at least put the company in a stronger position. And so, I went into super drive mode, working sixty-hour weeks to close the gap on our losses.

None of this explains why I quit.

I quit because I didn't want to be fired.

There, I said it. It doesn't sound great, but it's the truth. This tough nut didn't want to get canned.

Yes, there were warning signs from the beginning that something was amiss. Even before I came on board, there was a bait and switch with my job title. And then there was a bait and switch over who I would report to. My husband tried to tell me not to take the job, but I thought the opportunity was too good to pass up. Once I started, there were other signs.

"No one has ever voluntarily left the company," the HR director confided to me one afternoon. It was in the early days after my promotion during a Zoom check-in. Actually, she wasn't confiding so much as beaming with pride.

The company *did* have a welcoming, family-like atmosphere. Thanks to its flexible, remote work and offsite meetings in destinations like Orlando and Mexico, people didn't want to leave. But there was a lot of turnover. The problem with no one leaving by choice is that it creates a lot of uncertainty within the workforce, especially in the department that gets the most scrutiny.

I could sense the CEO had been cooling toward me. While I reported to him, we didn't meet often. Instead, I met with the chief operating officer, who served as a sort of go-between. A few months after my promotion, the CEO brought in his childhood best friend, a high-level marketing VP who had left the company he was working for. It was supposed to be a temporary arrangement so he could help build one of our marketing initiatives showing major promise, but after our leadership meeting in May, I was told that I would report to him.

Almost overnight, I felt like I went from being the savior of the company to persona non grata with the CEO. I might as well have not existed. It was like I was back in middle school getting my first B. It was devastating to feel like I wasn't respected or valued.

Now, I could have stayed the course. Outside of the CEO, I was praised for bringing more cohesion and transparency to the operation. My team was making progress toward our company's goal, although it still wasn't achievable within our timeframe. My actual chances of getting fired were low, but I didn't see any chance of turning around my relationship with the CEO. And I knew I would never have his support.

What I haven't said until now is that the entire time I was working for this company, one of my children was battling a life-threatening illness. Outside of work, I did my best to line up specialists, therapists, and psychiatrists.

One of the major fallouts of Covid has been a spike in mental health issues, including eating disorders. Anorexia cases had almost doubled in the first year of the pandemic, creating demand that led to significant delays in getting diagnoses and treatment. It took six months to get my child in to see an eating disorder specialist, who confirmed my suspicions.

We began an aggressive treatment plan, but it wasn't enough. So, we got on a waitlist for a partial hospitalization program or PHP. Once in, my child spent seven days a week, roughly nine a.m. to nine p.m. every day for the next four months. She was resistant at first, "white-knuckling it," as the therapists like to say. Eventually, she started making progress and decided she would do whatever it took to get out of the program so she could spend the last month of the semester back at school with her friends.

We were hopeful when she left treatment, but I wasn't expecting a complete recovery. My daughter stepped down from PHP not quite in her target weight range, which meant we would have to do it at home, outside of a clinical setting. Fortunately, we had a great team in place. Her nutritionist from the program had transitioned to private practice, so we could continue seeing her for weekly sessions. We also resumed sessions with the other specialists she had seen before she entered treatment, so there was continuity in her care. My daughter's weight and mood remained steady for a while, and my family returned to doing what it had always done, which was largely scrounging for dinner and eating solo.

You see, back when I had mapped out my carefully planned life, I had left off cooking dinner. This was the domain of stay-at-home moms. I intended to be a successful career woman.

I had spent a lifetime looking down on the dutiful mothers who prepared home-cooked meals that their families sat down to every night. I didn't realize that a major reason for my aversion was my own trauma. Dinner had been the scene of some of my father's most explosive tirades, almost always aimed at my mother. She was expected to perfectly execute every aspect of the meal, right down to serving. If something didn't go as planned—the gravy was too runny, or the chicken fried steak was overcooked—it was like a bomb detonating right there at the dinner table. And none of us would be spared.

When I was working full-time, it was easy to find excuses for why I couldn't cook. But by the time I quit my job, my daughter's weight was in free fall. Her eating disorder had been working behind the scenes, ensuring she was reducing portions on every meal or snack she ate. Outwardly, she proclaimed everything was fine. And then, almost overnight, everything imploded, and every single meal became an epic battle. There was revolting, yelling, crying, and sometimes outright refusal to eat. My child was no longer there. I was only dealing with a raging eating disorder that was hell-bent on never letting her eat without fear again.

Relapses are common, especially for eating disorders. From our early days in group meetings, my husband and I heard from parents whose kids had been in treatment for months, some of them for the second or third time. Relapse rates for patients with anorexia are typically between 35% to 41% in the first eighteen months. We wanted her to recover, so we had tough decisions to make. *Should we send her back to treatment? Should we double down on trying to refeed her undernourished body at home?* I knew from statistics that if not resolved, my child would likely die from this illness or a related complication. I didn't want that for her. *What would it take to defeat this illness once and for all?*

The answer was one I had been too scared to admit, but without the distraction of work, there were no more excuses. To help my daughter, I needed to address my own eating issues.

Now, I like to think no one saw me all these years, with my neurotic food rules, avoidance of certain foods, special diets, and need to exercise at all costs. I spent years trying to hide what I perceived as my unacceptable behavior, lack of control, and lack of willpower. I would beat myself up because I couldn't do the one thing I needed to do that would allow me to see myself as a success—which was to get down to an acceptable size. I didn't have an eating disorder, but I had disordered eating.

Research shows that caregivers who have their own issues around food can still support someone recovering from anorexia, but I felt like a fraud. I was carrying around my own shame. How could I ask my daughter to do something I was too afraid to do? When she shared with me that I could help her by eating with her, there was no question about what I needed to do. So, I delved into the research and best practices for caregivers refeeding teens with anorexia. Parents often play the most important role in a child's recovery. To date, the most successful treatment for eating disorders is family-based therapy, an intensive outpatient treatment method led by a parent or parents in consultation with specialists.

I put my energy into helping my daughter—actually my whole family—cooking and sitting down to regular dinners for the first time in my adult life. I went all in on refeeding my daughter, taking control of every aspect of her meals and snacks, planning, preparing, plating, and sitting down and eating with her six times a day, doing battle with her own demons and mine. For the first few weeks, every single meal or snack time was tense. Then we started making progress.

For myself, I began intuitive eating, an evidence-based, mind-body health approach that rejects diets and diet culture and promotes eating for satisfaction and satiety. It is also aligned with eating disorder treatment. The more I embraced the idea of intuitive eating, the more I realized my lifetime of body-shaming, dieting, overexercising, and overeating needed to end. It would mean addressing all the things that caused my eating issues in the first place—trauma, insecurity, having my self-worth tied to appearance, and living in a naturally larger body. It would take time—possibly years—to learn to eat intuitively, heal my relationship with food, and be okay with my body. I hired a therapist trained in intuitive eating because I knew I would have to deal with these emotions I had been trying to stuff down my entire existence. I also decided to document my journey—the struggles and the successes. In the early days of recovery, the seeds of my next career were being sown, although I was still too scared to voice it. I wanted to write a book about the experience.

Many experts can tell you *how* to eat intuitively, but few people will tell you *what it's really like* as you make the transition. I had so many questions, especially about what would happen to my body. Most dietitians won't answer these questions because intuitive eating is a framework for making peace with food, not a diet, and every person's experience is different.

For those who have never struggled with their weight or self-image, it's probably unfathomable how much weight and appearance can influence life decisions. But when you spend your time and energy feeling that you aren't a success or that you even deserve success, you limit yourself in every capacity.

I took a hard look at myself and examined the parts of me I didn't want to see. My safe, protective bubble, where I planned all my moves, had kept me from reaching my true potential. After giving up on dieting, I saw how I had let my feelings of inadequacy drive my decisions. I could never enjoy my successes because inside, I felt like it wasn't enough. I wasn't good enough because no matter how hard I tried, I was never within an acceptable range of thin.

Sometimes clarity comes in like a comet out of nowhere. It blazes a trail that started long before it was visible. When I quit my job, I had no idea what I would do with myself.

I had never *not* had a plan. I had never *not* known what would come next. But there was also this part of me that understood that if I could make it past the initial weeks of discomfort and use that time for introspection, I might find the courage to start something beautiful.

The scariest decision I ever made was to stop restricting myself and allow my body to be whatever size it was meant to be. I gave myself permission to eat what I wanted when I wanted. Without limits or judgment, I discovered I didn't need willpower to stop eating. Sometimes I ate more, and sometimes I ate less. I worked to stop judging and start listening. I started dismantling my negative self-image and using therapy to process my trauma. A few months in, the metaphorical weight came off my shoulders. Possibilities opened. I realized what I had always wanted was right in front of me. At my core, I had always dreamed of being a full-time author, and all of the work I had done before had prepared me for it. It was time to take the next step. So, I did.

KRISTI KOETER

Kristi is a marketing and communications leader with twenty years of experience as a journalist, author, editor, and digital strategist. She believes compelling content has the power to change lives.

As editor of the *Austin American-Statesman*'s websites, she steered coverage for Central Texas' biggest news stories. Under her leadership, Statesman.com won the Texas Associated Press Managing Editors' Best Online Newspaper in 2008, 2009, 2010, and 2012. At Undercover Tourist, a family travel agency, she established the content marketing program and grew blog traffic to one million page views *per month* by unraveling the secrets of Disney vacation planning.

She is working on her most personal project to date, a book chronicling her own quest to heal her relationship with food after a lifetime of dieting, restriction, and overexercising.

https://www.kristikoeter.com
https://www.linkedin.com/in/kristikoeter/
https://www.facebook.com/kristikoeter
https://www.instagram.com/kristikoeter/

3
DESTINED TO RUN

DIANA MALDONADO

W alking down the streets of my neighborhood in Eagle Pass, the border town I grew up in, brings me a sense of warmth and acceptance that I didn't fully appreciate when I was younger. The road was a lot smoother back then.

As a little girl, there was freedom in discovering a new world outside my barrio. One could say my adventure trekking began at the ripe age of six. Wandering through potholed streets, dirt roads, and trails, alone and with friends, I would venture to the neighborhood corner grocery store when my mom needed a loaf of bread, or I wanted a treat. I'd sneak into her coin drawer to get money from her seamstress work so I could buy some candy, and I felt so grown-up when I paid the grocer.

Every morning, my sister and I walked to school in our beautiful matching striped ponchos. On our walk, I would look down the street, stretch my eyes to where the street dead-ended, and get a glimpse of the school. As I passed each house on the way, I gave a thumbs-up to the houses I liked and wondered what it would be like to live in some of those houses because they were so nice with flowers and shrubbery—you could tell they had roots and stability.

Our house was a shoddy unleveled brick house with a vast dirt landscape of a lawn void of flowers and greenery. My family lived in a rental house, and all my friends owned their houses. I would fantasize about what it would be like to own our home as I walked to school. Not wanting to be late, I arrived with ample time before the school bell rang and to have enough time to play and say hi to my classmates. One can say I was already networking!

Whenever there was a school event or dance to attend, my four best friends, Isabel, Belinda, Maribel, Ari, and I, formed a system to walk together. I would start the process since I lived the farthest away. Zigzagging through the streets, I picked them up one by one until all five of us were together, and we'd set off on our outing. When the dance or event was over, we'd do the entire process in reverse. If it was getting late, as it often would because we were having fun walking together, I would have to run home. It felt a bit scary, but even more so exhilarating, knowing that I'd had fun exploring the streets and having a new adventure. Looking back, it was a pretty good safety support system because, as young as we were, we traveled as a group.

During the summers, my siblings—my older brother and my younger sister and brother—tagged along as we walked across the bridge connecting the US and Mexico for our annual visit to the dentist in Mexico. My father was friends with a dentist there, Dr. Tamez, who was cheaper than a dentist in the US. My father worked in San Antonio for most of my formative years due to his lack of formal education and a scarcity of jobs in Eagle Pass. To make ends meet, my mom took a factory job at the Dickies denim plant and quickly found a carpool with other ladies because she didn't know how to drive. So, while Mom carpooled off to work, we dutifully obeyed and made the trek to and from Mexico and sometimes stopped by the town square to get a snack on our way back home.

In the third grade, I got another taste of freedom when I got my first bike. My cool green bike took me further into the streets and off the walking paths I usually traversed. I convinced my friends to get bikes too, and off we went to new places, me leading our pack of fearless girls with the biggest smiles on our faces and the wind blowing through our hair. We invited other girls to join us—we ended up with a total of nine—and extended our trip to ride out to the outskirts of town to explore a creek. Off we went, or so we thought. The world was our taco, or, as some say, oyster! However, it proved to be longer and logistically challenging to explore when you have a long chain of bikes cluttering up the road. One of the girls ended up with a flat, so she had to ditch her bike on the side of the road and come back for it later. Luckily, she was able to ride with someone else. Thinking back, I'm not sure if they ever picked up the bike.

Throughout my life, the sense of adventure has been a humming bright light inside of me, encouraging me to push the boundaries and take that extra step to see what new surprises lay around the corner. Elders, teachers, neighbors, and peers came to know me as a leader with a sense of confident determination. I was once interviewed for a weekly student spotlight, and the teacher asked me what I wanted to be when I grew up. Without skipping a beat, I gleefully shouted, "A doctor!" The teacher gently reminded me that I should consider being a nurse because, "Diana, being a nurse is more appropriate for a girl." But I was adamant that I wanted to be a doctor, not a nurse. After several rounds of discussions, the article was written, and it was noted that although the teacher tried "convincing" me to be a nurse, she said, "Diana was adamant about her ambition to be a doctor."

Recently, I came across my fifth-grade report card and read the teacher's comments. She noted that I could read two grades above my grade level, I tutored my peers, I contributed to new ideas, and I expressed myself "exceptionally well in both Spanish and English." While she indicated that I could advance by two grade levels, she did not recommend it. Deflated with the possibility, I began to question my support system. With a lack of role models, sponsors, and relatable figures in my life, some wins became more elusive, and the stakes got more challenging as I got older. To be fair, I think the teacher wanted to go on record and say that I was capable of advancing, yet the system was not set up for this academic opportunity for me.

I could never have imagined what would lie ahead in my future and how my formative years gave me questions and answers, all at the same time. Curiosity, adventure, doubt, and fear were swirling inside me, and it felt like unraveling a mystery. Time would bring that all into perspective.

Getting pregnant at eighteen and marrying one week after high school sent my path in a different direction than the one I was originally on. As much as I valued my independence and being different, I became a cultural statistic. I saw my dreams of becoming a doctor dash away, and I disappointed my parents, a hurt that I felt and regretted deeply. I was their hope to break out of the cycle of poverty and into prosperity through my education. However, being the eternal optimist, I looked for ways to keep that dream in sight. Although I had become a statistic, I would make mine with an asterisk.

I enrolled in the local junior college and began my academic journey, and although it was very limited in class offerings, it was better than nothing. I still laugh when I remember trying to fit my pregnant belly into the traditional right-handed desks because being left-handed made for some interesting maneuvering. In my classes, I thrived, and it felt good! Yet my time in school was short-lived because of how life unfolded for me as a young mother with other important responsibilities. And I truly believe my son, Alex, was learning alongside me because he went on to be enrolled in the gifted and talented programs throughout his academic years.

In my twenties, I loved the experience of being a young mom to Alex and Denise. I enjoyed filling my kids' worlds with excitement, especially living in Austin, because there was so much more to offer than the small town I grew up in. Denise has the distinguished title of being the native Austinite in the family! Some of my siblings had already settled in California, allowing us to spend summers on the beaches, take trips to zoos and theme parks, and travel the iconic

Highway 101 from San Diego, LA, Monterey, and all the way up to San Francisco. As my extended family continued to expand and move to different parts beyond the border town walls, we traveled into Mexico, visiting Saltillo and Monterrey, and I experienced a totally new appreciation of my heritage and culture.

As life continued to settle in Austin and take on a routine of its own, life was secure and happy. Guiding my kids in school and being mindful of playing an active role in their education led me to advocate and be a voice for other students and parents through PTA work and translating for parents. It felt like a calling, and it was gratifying to find a new joy and purpose. I loved seeing the excitement in my kids when they had a new adventure, and I longed for new adventures, too. However, as the years passed, I drove past the local university on my way to work every morning. It felt like déjà vu from when I used to walk down the street during my elementary years fantasizing about big dreams. I often thought about getting my degree, which was still a dream unfulfilled. But with work and family responsibilities, I kept driving to work, and it would quickly vanish from my thoughts. However, the dream of returning to college and getting my degree started to resurface, and I dusted off the layers of cobwebs as the idea became more central in my mind. The idea would not let me rest. The persistent but patient and forgiving voice kept reminding me to make room for this possibility, and I would soon come to the realization that I wanted this more than ever.

Bringing a seventeen-year marriage to an end was one of the most difficult decisions of my life. As I pondered what was on the horizon for the rest of my life, I wondered if I could fathom living another seventeen years unhappy or if I should chart a new path, one that was not guaranteed and, in fact, potentially more stressful and challenging. Here was another statistic upon me—single mothers are often in poverty—so I worked hard to make sure that didn't happen because, again, I was determined not to be a statistic. I owed this to my kids, not to myself. They deserve better, and I wasn't going to fail them. My path forward was for me to finish the college education I had started sixteen years prior. Once I earned my degree, I would be able to provide for my kids—give them opportunities, gain the freedom to level up to new places, and settle the score by honoring that dream I'd had as a little girl. As you can imagine, it was a chaotic time in my life as I immersed myself in evening courses while working full-time and being a mom to a teen and a preteen. Many sacrifices were made along the way, and I said "no" to invites and even family gatherings because time was such a precious commodity. My mom and sister were nearby to help, but I give my kids a lot of credit as they sacrificed the most during that time.

Because I was laser-focused, I asked my school advisor what the shortest time possible for me to graduate was. Time was ticking, and I would not lose another second in this fleeting moment. I was one of the oldest students in my cohort, which initially was embarrassing but would be to my advantage in the long run. Because of my work experience, I could share with my fellow students what I'd learned beyond classroom theory, which broadened the learning component for my younger peers. Through the program, I submitted portfolios on my lived work experience to earn course credit. I ended up placing out of twelve hours of Spanish on a placement test. Having a limited income meant I didn't have a computer at home, so after church on Sundays, I would drop off the kids at my mom's house, head to the local library, and spend three to four hours there.

As the pace of school progressed, I overheard my cohort talking about their GPA and became curious about what mine was. Having layers of multiple priorities on my plate was a lot. Between my full-time job supervising a dozen employees, finalizing my divorce, being a single parent, managing a household budget, studying, and checking off the credit hours I'd earned, it was all I could take, or so I thought. My fellow students were striving to graduate with honors, so I looked at what grades I had accumulated and realized I was onto something. Not that I needed another priority, but what if? Pressing on, I charted another path of leveling up to the possibility of not just graduating but graduating with honors.

After going to school for five semesters straight without a break, I graduated with honors, magna cum laude in business administration and management. What started as a dream in 1981, I was finally able to achieve in 2000. The dream was so much richer to me because I had worked so hard for so many years, and I could appreciate it more. I was grateful to be surrounded by family and many people who saw me through my dream. While I didn't become a doctor, I healed from the regret I felt and made peace with the decisions and consequences that had haunted me for almost two decades. In spite of all this, that voice inside of me never gave up and was nudging me to my true calling—to be a voice for others and help people be a better version of themselves because I didn't have this at times when I most needed it. It felt good to have a foothold of certainty that I had earned, and I wouldn't change it for the world.

My plan was to spend time with my family and breathe, hoping to take a break after an arduous two years. I was basking on this highlight in my life, and things were tranquil, and I cherished every moment. Two years after I graduated, I got a phone call that changed my trajectory. There was a long-standing group of local Latino leaders, whom I didn't know were looking for fresh leaders to support in school board and municipal races, and they asked if I would come to a meeting. I didn't think anything of it because it wasn't in my periphery. But at the meeting, the moment presented itself for me to consider running for elected office. The little girl from the barrio looking for an adventure came alive again while my heart started beating faster because I was oh so afraid. This is out there! Growing up, I remember not having a mentor and having to figure things out on my own. I recall thinking that when I grew up, I would be a voice for others. No child should have to go through their education alone. Kids need mentors and support. I made a promise to be that voice one day.

As things panned out, the Latino leaders agreed that I would be the best candidate to run for the school board. I had no idea this would be another adventure in my journey where everything was so foreign, and there were no guardrails. But it brought me back to the idea of being a voice for students whose parents couldn't be engaged in their children's lives because they were working. When I spoke to my mom about it, she calmly and proudly encouraged me. She knew it was destined, and her demeanor gave me the fortitude to say yes. I don't think I could have done it without the experience of my lengthy education journey. It was the building block of leveling up, giving me the confidence I needed for my campaign: having to talk to strangers, both supporters and non-supporters, bringing a voice to students in my school district, and even giving others the dream of an education who might not think it was for them. I also lived in Round Rock, a conservative suburb north of Austin, which now had a lot of white people due to white flight when Austin began to diversify several years back. I was fairly new to Round Rock and didn't have a lot of representation of people who looked like me, so belonging was important. But I worked hard to campaign and win the trust of the voters. In 2003, I was elected to office and took that responsibility to heart. Sitting on the school board dais was the beginning of more challenges, but great opportunities were ahead. The little girl's voice inside me was getting stronger and louder—it was an awakening or a rebirth.

Re-election came around in 2006, and I shared with close friends that I wanted to win with 80% of the vote, given that I had won with 65% in the first go-round. My friends chuckled and suggested that because it was still predominantly white, I shouldn't cast my nets too far and that getting over 50% was a good win.

It reminded me of the teacher who suggested I become a nurse. Their comments didn't change what I did, but they stayed in my mind subliminally and incentivized me to work hard because, as an incumbent, it was my race to lose. On election night, the results came in at 79.4%, and many doubters went away.

While the school board had many successes early on, there were long meetings and nights spent working due to setbacks in education funding. At times, it seemed we were going in circles and getting nowhere. I questioned if I was making any impact, and quite frankly, I was becoming disillusioned.

At an evening gala for public education, a political party leader who was my guest started a conversation with a small group and was at the crux of identifying a leader in the community to run as the Democratic candidate for state office in a conservative Republican district. Another guy in the group, who was active in the community, was beaming because he felt it would be him. But as we kept talking, it became apparent to the party leader that the answer was right under his nose—me! Giddy with his newfound answer, he left the function, and the legwork began for me to run for state office. And the guy who wanted to run got upset, and I told him, "Go ahead and run, and may the best woman win."

The journey to this unknown universe unfolded organically. However, it came with a steep learning curve. In August 2007, I hadn't yet announced my candidacy because the filing window didn't open until December. The leadership at the state agency where I worked caught wind of me possibly running and brought me in to inquire about my plans and basically tried to bully me into not running by threatening me. The day after I officially filed to run for office, I was fired from my job. After a career of over two decades, in which I had an exemplary track record and won numerous awards, they let me go because I was now running for office with the opposite political party. As a single parent, I was the only one earning an income, so this was a devastating blow. They knew what they were doing and came at me hard, and there were more obstacles I would encounter down the road. Scared and anxious, I began questioning myself. Without a stable income, did I want to put my family through this? What else lies ahead that I will have to figure out? Was this the end of my journey—the voice I'd fought so hard for to help others? Scurrying to my car in the parking garage one day, I called my best friend, Socorro, who had experience with campaigns and had been by my side since we first met in 1994. When I finished purging all my fears and doubts, she calmly put the picture together, reminding me why I was doing this.

She said, "Now, put on your big girl panties and go out there and win." I vowed to win with more fervor.

With the campaign in full blast, I was getting bombarded from different directions, and it felt like I was swimming upstream. However, I had a great team, and without their expertise, I couldn't have pulled through. In fact, even with the layers of experience on my team, we were all learning new strategies because this hadn't been done before. We were in pretty deep, and as I realized what I was up against, I started playing mind games and envisioning the outcome. For every door I knocked on and got a no, I vowed to find five yeses—which meant a lot of walking and talking. I learned at a granular level the intricacies of block walking, voter tendencies, persuasion points and discussions, and marketing. A lot more goes on in an election behind the stump speeches and TV ads. I remember dialing for dollars in a small quirky room that felt like a closet with grim yellow lighting and was filled with dead crickets. However, the most humbling experience was seeing, day after day, the influx of people, most of them strangers, who would open the door to help me win. Pensively, this was much bigger than me—it was a belief, a cause, and a voice much, much greater than mine.

Fifteen months of campaigning was one of the most transformational periods in my life and more than what I had bargained for. I met and spoke with so many people all over the state and even nationally because so much was at stake. It was the first combined million-dollar race for a state seat, and that level of fundraising typically aligns more with congressional seats. Looking back, I was blissfully naïve to many of the nuances, but I know that helped me stay hyper-focused on winning. When the dust settled, the race ended up being one of the top three in that election cycle, and I made history as the first Latina, person of color, and female to win the seat.

Opening day in January 2009 was the culmination of that little girl who grew up in a border town barrio, walking down the long stretch of the street that dead-ended at her school, now standing honorably in the hollowed Texas House chamber. I looked around at the beauty and history surrounding me and wondered about the multitude of decisions that had been debated in that room. The excitement was electrifying, yet I had a stillness inside me, and my eyes welled up for a moment. Reflecting back, the road was not quite so smooth to begin with, but the lesson was to remain curious about what was in front of me. Following that curiosity led me to generate ideas and opportunities that beckoned me to ask for help and use my voice wisely. The journey brought joy, failures, wins, and lessons. Together, these experiences led me to know my value, honor my worth, and reminded me that things would be okay after all. In the end, I learned to forgive to myself and to have fun with the journey.

Ready to be sworn in, I raised my hand for my kids, my parents, my students, the dedicated volunteers who believed in me, and the countless voices who go unheard day after day, decade after decade, and even generation after generation. The little girl with her bright striped poncho made it to her destination.

DIANA MALDONADO

Diana Maldonado is an extraordinary contributor who leads with grace and purpose as CEO of Maldonado Strategies. In her expansive career as a long-time Austin political and public figure, her sharp insight for pinpointing incongruencies, combined with her method for listening and collaborating, helps organizations design and implement innovative solutions to accelerate their big vision goals and become the leading edge.

As the first Latina elected to represent Williamson County in the Texas House of Representatives and a leading voice in the political space, Diana has an established record for accomplishing the "impossible" while building lasting relationships. She is passionate about helping more women decode the process of running for office —and succeeding when they get there.

Diana is a global marathon runner, goes on travel hiking excursions, is a feng shui enthusiast, and loves spending time with her three-year-old granddaughter, Camila.

https://www.maldonadostrategies.com/
https://www.facebook.com/diana.maldonado.39566
https://www.instagram.com/dianamaldonado7755/
https://www.linkedin.com/in/diana-maldonado/

4

A YEAR ALONE

CHRISTY JAYNES

T he sun was coming up as I started my car, and on a random Spotify station, the Avett Brothers sang, "Load the car and write the note…" while my husband stood beside the car looking at me with deep sadness—there wasn't too much to say. This was a "see you later, not a goodbye," but it felt like something so much more painful. Greater forces were at work, and this moment was devastating and liberating all at once.

As I drove east toward the rising sun, the next song began to play—Counting Crows, the song, "A Long December"…

> A long December and there's reason to believe
> Maybe this year will be better than the last
> I can't remember the last thing that you said as you were
>   leavin'…
> It was December…and I was leaving.

I was driving to my new home twenty-three hours away. Car packed with my essentials: a computer, a suitcase full of clothes, bedding, towels, a basket of kitchen basics, a string of holiday lights…all the things it would take to create small moments of joy as I rebuilt my life in a new space, slept on the floor, and waited for my moving truck to arrive. I've always loved movies where a woman breaks free from a difficult situation and recreates her life in a whole new way. Stories where small wins bring meaning to a fresh and uncertain start. And that's exactly where I found myself.

After three days, I pulled into my driveway, but not before I made a quick stop for some basic supplies: a Christmas wreath, cheese, wine, coffee, milk, and a lovely and unexpected bundle of flowers from my cashier as a "Welcome to Saint Louis" gift. I got out, stretched my legs, and stood before my beautiful front door—a stripped and waxed reclaimed antique door that had caught my eye when I scrolled through possible new homes on the internet. I found out later that the door had been rescued and installed by my neighbor Andy, who, shortly after my arrival, knocked on it, along with his wife Becky and their five children, each clutching a small welcome gift in their hands: a lemon, some homemade cookies, a loaf of bread, eggs from their chickens, and flowers. How did Saint Louis already know I love flowers? This would not be the last time my new neighbors showered me with love and kindness in a way that made me cry like people cry when they are truly seen and celebrated for who they are.

I'd never been to Missouri, but after several years of looking at cities in the Midwest, I decided that Saint Louis embodied all the qualities I was hoping for in a new town—great food, music, architecture, a rich history, and natural beauty. The house I found online would be a safe haven, a new start, a promise of a better future. At 126 years old, it came with its own set of challenges, but also character and so much potential. I slowly painted rooms and planned my projects. The daily joy I found felt triumphant in its honesty and simplicity.

Even fresh starts come with challenges, and over the next few months, I would experience my entire moving truck full of my most important belongings being stolen, discarded without any communication, and then miraculously found by a stranger and finally reclaimed. During this challenging time, I came to terms with what it meant to lose everything I thought was my life: photos, art, books, and all of the functional tools that made my life a little easier and more enjoyable. I had always wondered how people endured the devastation of losing everything after a fire or flood…this was sort of like that, only with the smack of disdain I felt for the people who chose to do this to someone as their livelihood. In the end, I came to a sort of peace around the loss and began to love the minimalism of slowly rebuilding my home in an intentional way. Then one day, amazingly, a stranger messaged me that they had found my stuff. They, too, had lost their belongings in the moving scam. Somehow this woman's fiancé had found both of our truckloads in a random storage unit, waiting to be auctioned or dumped or sold. I scrambled to make arrangements to reclaim my boxes and furniture. Six months after arriving at my new place, my things finally made it home. I had surrendered, and the universe delivered a miracle.

Spring brought lots of new projects, both at my new home and in my life. As a way to ground myself in this new life, I joined a 100-Day Challenge to produce a piece of art every day for 100 days. By combining my original paintings with hundreds of digital images, I created collages that were organic and sometimes absurd, but all born of a deeply relaxing process that was a combination of meditation and play. After posting my art on Instagram, enough people showed interest in purchasing prints, so I put it all on my website for sale. Each piece was a little story, and the fact that others enjoyed them made the project even richer.

I bought mail-order day-old baby chicks, raised them in a puppy pool in my kitchen, and then converted an old shed near the garden into a chicken coop. My first-year garden was a mixed success. For the chickens, it was a huge success, as they escaped their pen and dined on most of the harvest before it was even picked. As I learned about growing things in a new part of the country and brought life to this old yard, I could feel myself unwinding, opening, and releasing.

My first summer was a blur of friends and family visiting, sharing delicious meals, and exploring my new city together. Record rains flooded my basement with six inches of water, enough to destroy lots of my stuff and break the furnace. Couple that with a broken air conditioner, and most of my decorative plans turned into repair plans. Starting in July, Saint Louis becomes hot, wet, steamy, and full of bugs. The best part of summer was that it ended right on time.

On the first day of autumn, the temperatures dropped, the air cleared, and everything shifted, including me. The noise of stress upon stress had been keeping me ungrounded. Now, between each new experience was the silence of being alone, a stillness that permeated each room, each hour, and it seeped into my bones. Life's rhythms had slowed to an almost imperceptible beat, and it was there that I met the demons who had been haunting me for years, and there were a few.

THE DEMONS

Sometimes a great decline comes after a particularly high point in life. As a self-employed entrepreneur for over a decade, I'd had my share of successes. I created online businesses, opened brick-and-mortar shops, and helped others do the same through coaching and consulting. I'd led civic projects, won grants, and created events that small businesses and locals still enjoy today. My shops were very popular and received lots of coverage in the news and in magazines. In my coaching practice, I'd guided people into realizing some very big dreams. I was recognized for my work and was invited to be interviewed on radio shows and blogs. I'd worked for the love of it, and people loved my work. I was in heaven.

As for my demons, well, even with all my successes, those began to chip away at me after going through a divorce that was shockingly foul. I was not prepared for the social warfare that was waged by my ex-husband. A quiet uncoupling is what I wanted—telling people, "He was great, but we just had too many differences," was my party line. The truth was, he was emotionally abusive behind closed doors —in a pattern of cruelty and love bombing, he would keep things unstable and unhealthy. His favorite currency was lies, even about

46

mundane things that didn't matter. He fabricated stories about me and sprinkled them throughout our community like confetti. This lack of integrity, and lack of respect, ate away at me. I just had to get out; I wanted to slip away quietly, but he wanted me to slip in my own proverbial blood on the way out. While he was never physical, he definitely did all he could to destroy me, for years. And while this was definitely my bumpiest road yet, it wasn't until one October evening when I was brutally assaulted by a man I had been casually dating that the slow descent into dysfunction began.

Being a single mom, I had no time for trauma and needed to keep things moving forward since there was no safety net. So, after ten days of a liquid diet and bed rest, I went back to work. Then, after the bruising disappeared, I tried to jump back into dating. I slapped on a smile to celebrate the holidays and expanded my coaching business with an "I can do whatever I want" attitude. I went on to open another successful store after that, but the entire time I was shrinking into my dysfunction. I thought I could out-think trauma and summon the strength to leave it in the dust, but I didn't understand what trauma was. My divorce undid me and left me traumatized and socially alienated, but the physical trauma of the assault seeded itself in my body, settled under my skin, and began to take hold of me in ways I could not understand at the time.

Life is never all good or all bad. While I declined, good things happened, too. I met a lovely man, and we lived in my cute little house for nearly a year before the owner decided to take advantage of the great San Diego housing market and sell it. While we looked for our next spot, we put everything in storage and stayed with his parents for what was supposed to be a short time. It became evident that his parents needed our help, and while I continued to look for a place for us, my boyfriend decided he was needed there and stopped entertaining the idea of finding a new place. In his heart, caring for his parents was a priority. I understood, and I was also stuck. This was definitely not where I wanted to be, yet something about slowing down, taking care of someone else, and tending to a home in need of love seemed like it could offer me a moment to catch my breath from years of holding myself together and marching forward. After many months of resisting, I decided to surrender and stay on board with my boyfriend at his parents' house. This decision would require me to reallocate my energy so I could show up and be more present in caregiving and with the people I cared about. I've learned as an entrepreneur that if I've succeeded once, I can do it again, and sometimes it's okay to step away to take care of myself. I sold my store. I wound down my design and coaching businesses and decided to spend a semester in school.

During that semester, I got pneumonia a few weeks in, only to recover and become a full-time hospice caregiver for my boyfriend's stepdad, who quite suddenly passed away from cancer. Despite these setbacks, I worked hard and did well.

When that semester was over, I became a full-time caregiver to my boyfriend's mother. Alzheimer's and diabetes were two formidable diagnoses that had been left unchecked for a good while. Because of his own health struggles, her husband had not been able to care for her, or maybe he wasn't willing to admit how bad their health challenges really were. Now it was time for us to clean up the messes that neglect and dementia can do to a life, a home, a body, a bank account. We had our work cut out for us. Little did I know that being her caregiver would wear on me for years.

Trauma has a funny way of moving in and remodeling our lives in covert ways. Over the next several years, the bottom dropped out of my life in such a way that I hardly recognized myself. I gained seventy pounds, my hair started falling out, and I had several visits to the ER with mystery ailments. It took enormous effort to get to a place of feeling any kind of inspiration. And in between each moment of distress, I tried to take care of myself—I arranged flowers, made healthy meals, read and listened to books that lifted me up, meditated, and went on long walks in the canyon near our home. In a simple courthouse ceremony, my boyfriend became my husband. We planted a garden—a beautiful garden full of fruits, vegetables, herbs, and flowers. I found shady places for naps and created spaces for gathering together to eat and celebrate life. I made peace with the elements of loss I felt around my businesses and divorce. And still…I deteriorated.

By the time the pandemic started, I was already worn down and unsure how to move forward in our situation—dealing with unchecked trauma while caregiving is not a winning combo. Living out of a small bedroom with all my possessions in storage took a toll on me and felt indefinitely temporary. In addition, there's a phenomenon where family members find comfort in the denial of how bad an illness is and then critique the people who show up 24/7 to care for their loved one. My situation was very much that way. Sacrifice, coupled with critique and the fact that I was the one contorting myself to fit into this house and into this family, all left me empty. No one was bending to help me feel like I belonged. Maybe I didn't belong.

Mid-pandemic, I figured I'd do another quarter of college online to keep my mind busy. I started a rigorous full-time schedule at the University of Washington and dove in completely. And then one day, midway through the quarter, something happened, and I can't even tell you why or how. I saw myself from outside, and I had lost my grip, and there was not a single branch or foothold on the way down. And so, with my last bit of energy, I emailed each professor and withdrew from my classes, far too late into the semester to get a refund on tuition and with an A+ standing. The next day I went to the emergency room with terrible stomach pains, and a few days after that, I went again. While one doctor felt there was something very wrong that had nothing to do with my stomach complaints, they couldn't quite nail the problem. They kept asking me if I felt safe at home…they were on the right track but had the wrong reasons. I felt physically safe at home, but I did not feel sane; I did not feel emotionally well. Another doctor toyed with keeping me for observation and respite but, in the end, couldn't justify it and sent me back home. Why didn't I speak up? Why didn't I say, "I think I'm losing my mind?" I knew that's why I was there, but I couldn't say the words. On top of caregiving in an unsupportive environment during a pandemic, my trauma was all too much.

Later that summer, I reached the bottom of my despair and was forced to contemplate drastic alternatives. Since I am an entrepreneur, a drastic alternative looks a lot like a win-win solution with a financially sound foundation and potential for growth for all those involved. I presented plan A to my husband, a plan to move into a home with space for the three of us, his mom, him, and me, to live comfortably and sustainably for the coming years. He was enthusiastic until we got such immense pushback from his mother and her family that he couldn't support my plan anymore. My plan B was to leave. Not divorce my husband, but move to a new space to regain my health. I hoped that, somehow, he would be able to join me in a fresh start sooner than later.

I've lived all around the country—Washington, Montana, Virginia, Texas, California—but never in the Midwest. I've always loved the people I met from the Midwest and figured it was time to give the middle of the country a try. Saint Louis had been on my radar for years, not for her sterling crime rates, ahem, but for all of the amazing food, culture, architecture, and natural beauty. I had a tight budget and a big dream, and I found a house online that spoke to my heart. That was it. It's amazing how once we make up our minds about something that sparks us, seemingly impossible things begin to line up and light the way forward. The strength of that "yes" moment set everything in motion. I said yes to this big old house, I said yes to Saint Louis, I said yes to myself.

I arrived in my new city three days before my forty-ninth birthday, two weeks before Christmas, with just enough time before the start of a new year to make some pretty big resolutions. In the end, I didn't lose the weight, or replace the old windows, or finish creating the best-ever guest room (I'm big into hospitality). I didn't create a thriving art business, just a humble little one. What did I accomplish? I spent time watching squirrels, chickens, and cardinals in my yard. I cultivated a magical friendship with the family next door that grew into sharing meals and holidays, birthdays, struggles, and wins. We show up for one another in a way that feels like how I'd imagine the writers of TV shows about two next-door neighbors imagine they're portraying their characters. And I have acknowledged my inability to meet life and run with her while calling that dysfunction what it is, a deep trauma. A trauma that will heal so long as I continue to shine a light on it and be kind to myself —not internet-branded self-care, but true compassion and forgiveness for all I have perceived as shortcomings and refocusing my thoughts through a new lens that reveals…it's not my fault. I spent my entire autumn learning about trauma, seeking therapies, and allowing myself space to heal. The top of my mountain in life wasn't achieving something beautiful, or successful, or profitable…it was finally allowing the silence to swallow me whole and to face what came up in the dark head-on so that I might know real freedom.

Today, I know that living well means finding beauty in the mundane moments each day. This is my key to success, peace, and ultimately my inspiration to start anew. I've always told my coaching clients that success is joy in the tiniest moments on the way to your goals and that the moment of realization that you've reached a goal has the same value as every other moment of each day. Does that reduce the value of reaching our goals? No, I don't think so. It increases the value of our daily lives. With this mindset, we open our eyes to the potential around us and find that, very often, we already have everything we need. We realize that to have a big goal is a privilege—not work but play—and that's a lovely place to be.

As I wrote this story, I wondered, what song would I close with? I opened with songs that captured the moment and showed up right on time. What have I been listening to this year that could convey the pain and joy on this life path and emphasize that the choices we make to be true to ourselves are the biggest decisions we'll ever make? There was only one choice, not a song, but a collection of songs, The Ballad of Cleopatra, by The Lumineers. There's an amazing video that ties the songs together on YouTube. It's a good twenty-four minutes and captures the beauty of bittersweetness and the importance of breaking free…

Pack yourself a toothbrush, dear
Pack yourself a favorite blouse
Take a withdrawal slip
Take all of your savings out
'Cause if we don't leave this town
We might never make it out
I was not born to drown
Baby, come on
"Sleep On The Floor,"
— The Lumineers

What do you need to break free from to become your truest self? Yeah, you. What is the heaviest weight on your chest, the one keeping you from moving in the direction that lights you up and delivers endless tiny moments of joy tucked into the fabric of everyday life? There's no need to drown, we can climb up to the light, and we can climb toward joy one moment at a time. That's my work, that's my success. Maybe you'll join me. Baby, come on.

CHRISTY JAYNES

Christy coaches women who find themselves at a turning point in life, helping them take authentic steps toward real goals that end up looking a lot like the life they've dreamed of. Her highly individualized approach focuses on meeting her clients right where they are and helping them to actively create what's next.

As an entrepreneur, community activist, and artist, she has imagined and realized businesses, events, and meaningful solutions for her clients while balancing life as a mother and wife and through her own journey of self-development.

A year ago, she moved from California to St Louis, Missouri, where she's remodeling an old house she bought off the internet. Knee-deep in projects, she lives with ten chickens and a small one-eyed dog named Jack.

https://www.instagram.com/christyjaynesart/
https://www.facebook.com/christy.s.jaynes
https://www.linkedin.com/in/christy-jaynes-a3740814/

5
HOT POTATO

MEG HAYS

As I added one more line to my resume, which was already full of nine-month to three-year gigs, I wondered, "What the hell is wrong with me? Why can't any of these career paths stick?"

The laundry list of jobs resembled that of a quitter, instead of the accomplished entrepreneur I had always dreamed of becoming. I had worked as a productivity coach, real estate assistant, pool company marketeer, and homebuilder project manager, which rounded out to be a job per year! In essence, I let down four employers who counted on me to help their businesses grow, thrive, and accomplish great things. I wasn't affecting my own bottom line, but I was surely disrupting someone else's.

I was all over the place. I hopped around like a hot potato because none of these positions fit. I felt like a fish out of water in every single one of them. I wasn't making millions, and I detested not having the flexibility to spend time with my kids. I was deflated, defeated, and depressed.

In the previous years, I had attempted several of my own entrepreneur opportunities, but those hadn't lasted either. The view into my past revealed my compulsion to try something new, jump in with both feet, tread water for a bit, and then run out of steam. Ultimately, I would swim to shore because I was drowning in one way or another.

Would I ever find something that fed my soul, made money, and provided me the opportunity to be the mother I dreamed of being for my two boys? Each line of that resume told me the answer was no.

As I looked at every item on that sheet of paper, I realized I had learned something from each new possibility. And that's what they were—possibilities to lead me to a goal I wanted to reach, a dream I wanted to bring to fruition, and a passion that was on the cusp of breaking through.

It wasn't until February 2020—thirty years after graduating high school—that I really started to figure out what I wanted to be when I grew up. At that time, I began to contemplate where I had been, where I wanted to go, and how to formulate a path to get there. I finally reached a point in my life where I was no longer satisfied trying new things, only to give up.

I was tired of talking to myself in a way that I would never allow someone else to speak to me. The common themes running through my head were that I wasn't worthy, I was stupid, I would never be good at anything, and I definitely didn't have what it took to be a successful businesswoman. It was quite the aha moment when I figured out that every negative word I spoke to and about myself would be another brick in the wall that I was building between me and my dreams.

My moment of enlightenment didn't just drop out of thin air. It was an accumulation of years of counseling, hard work, setbacks, problems, self-development books, business coaches, podcasts, YouTube videos, and much more. My turning point in 2020 came when I began to feed my body nutritiously and my mind with positivity. These two elements combined to help me review my past and dream of my future with a clear mind.

Growing up, I had grandiose ideas of becoming a multi-millionaire as an entertainer, business owner, or president of a bank. President of a bank? Where did that come from? Guess it sounded cool at the time to my fifteen-year-old self.

My reality was that I graduated college, worked as a reporter for a local newspaper in small-town Tennessee, and bided my time until my then-boyfriend asked me to marry him, and I moved to Austin, Texas, where he was working in the tech industry. Yep, I was one of those girls who thought my life wouldn't begin until I was married. Yes, I was ambitious and a dreamer, but I honestly thought nothing would start until I settled down. I look at that young girl now and wonder what she was thinking. The silver lining to a very outdated viewpoint is that I married my soul partner, and I wouldn't change that detail for any success or money in the world.

Of course, once I was with the love of my life, I realized I hadn't considered what Meg wanted to do with her future. Until then, I had been working so hard to do what others deemed as the "right things" in life (e.g., making good grades, being a good person, finding a good husband) that I hadn't dug deep into my soul for a purpose and passion that would propel me into the life of literary awards, Fortune 500 listings, and the "Most Powerful Women in the World" accolades that, as a teenager, I had always thought would be in my future. Somewhere along the way, between college and especially in those first few years of my career path, I lost the vision and the confidence that I could do great things. Additionally, I found myself thinking that if I wasn't an award-winning "something," I wasn't good enough anyway.

Make no mistake, I have always had truckloads of ideas, dreams, and goals of a successful career in whatever is flopping my mop at the time. And, as my resume indicates with its fourteen items, including a plethora of positions at local companies and entrepreneurial adventures, I have never lacked the courage to jump ship and try something new. But just because you jump into the ocean from a burning ship, it doesn't mean there won't be large sharks waiting to eat you in the water.

A pivotal point in my life was having children in the midst of trying to find myself. I attempted many things that would lead me to the successful career I desired. At the time, I was a top producer in the real estate industry. I had worked extremely hard to get my license within six weeks and then build my clientele through marketing, networking, and plain old hard work. Without children, I loved being a realtor and was happy with my success. With children…not so much.

The addition of these two precious boys was a huge blessing in my life, but it also meant that my time was no longer my own. The thought of leaving them to go to work and missing a momentous occasion or first step was abhorrent. However, the idea that I wasn't contributing financially or being creative was just as appalling.

Before kids, I was proud of my marketing career with two internet startups and then in my thriving real estate business. In each of these professions, I received many kudos and awards for my accomplishments, and I believed I was on my way to an income that would make me *feel* successful, independent, and worthy of the honors.

Though grateful for these opportunities, I still felt like an adolescent floundering with who and what she wanted to become. It's like I was fooling those around me, along with the person in the mirror, that I was a winner when at my core, I felt like a fraud because I hadn't achieved more. I looked around and saw so many contemporaries making substantial amounts of money and being promoted up the ladder to positions I thought would have been mine by this time in my journey. The problem is that I wasn't sure I was even on the right ladder.

They say comparison is the killer of joy, and whoever "they" are is spot on!

Then came these darling boys. They were adorable, snuggly, and stole my heart from the get-go. They were also a ton of work. I was able to swing the jobs of mother-of-one and real estate agent pretty well, but then when child number two came along, everything changed. I closed on my last property listing at three p.m. on July 16, 2007, picked up the for-sale sign at seven p.m. that evening, and went into labor at nine p.m. At one o'clock in the morning of July 17, we welcomed our second son into the world. High on love for my new baby and the shock of now having to care for two little humans, I shut down my real estate business. Effective immediately.

Ocean, meet Meg. Again.

It's not like I had planned to quit my real estate career after having children, but I just didn't seem to have the drive to work hard on my career and be the best mom I could be. The decision devastated me, but I couldn't shake the dread of returning to work. To make matters even more stressful, my husband was annoyed that we were going from a two-income family of four to just one income…his. His reaction was completely valid, considering I had told him for years that I would never quit working, so he wouldn't have to worry about being our sole provider. My "will always work" proclamation was not made from a dishonest heart. I sincerely believed I would be a career woman, whether we had children or not. I guess it would be apropos to say "never say never."

Unable to do it all, I began doubting my capabilities and shaming myself because I lacked the skill to be a "wonder woman" like so many influencers indicated women could and should be. I was once again trying to "fake it until I made it" and was digging myself into a deep hole of loneliness and despair.

The first few years of motherhood were the most difficult. The mommying was the easy part. I truly believed I wasn't successful because I was "just" a mom. I started questioning, judging, and degrading my character because I was disappointed in myself for not being capable of more.

Okay, this is where I want to call bullshit. Motherhood is the toughest and most demanding job I have ever had. It's also the most-needed responsibility in the world because we are forming the characters of humans and are in charge of their well-being! No one should ever disparage a woman for choosing to raise children full-time or work while raising children. It does not matter which option the mother chooses: to be a stay-at-home mom and or a career mom. I guarantee both love their children deeply and only want the best for them. Each choice has its pros and cons, and no one's opinion counts or matters except for the parents of said children. Rant over.

As a new mother, contentment eluded me, and I slipped into a depression riddled with anxiety. The more I tried to make others around me happy, the further I sank. Of course, I cared for my family to the best of my ability, but at the price of not caring for myself.

The funny part is that housework, crafting, and being integrated into mom groups weren't really my thing, either. Instead of attending Mommy and Me classes, I just played with my kids and had playdates with my friends and their kids so we could have cocktails and lunch. My friends and I would pull my Walmart kiddie pool into my front yard and sunbathe while the kids played in the water. Such fun memories, but this only magnified my opinion that I lacked motherhood skills, as well as the skill to have a profession that made my dreams come true.

As most of you would probably agree, we are our biggest critics.

Four years into being a full-time stay-at-home mom, my dad was diagnosed with mesothelioma cancer. Thankfully, I was able to travel between Texas and Tennessee often during the last eighteen months of his life to help take care of him. I wouldn't have been able to do this had I been required to go to a job every day. These months included some of the most unforgettable moments in my life. Even with the difficulty of caring for a sick parent, I deeply enjoyed each day we spent together. I learned how to appreciate every single second with the ones we are blessed to have in this life.

Throughout my life, my dad was my hero, confidant, and always the parent I called for every celebration and disappointment. We had really bonded when I became a real estate agent because he loved being a real estate broker and was ecstatic that I was following in his path. My dad was the quintessential entrepreneur who owned his own brokerage company and held a real estate license in three states, but he owned several other companies throughout his lifetime. His business journey started when he bought his first printing company at the wee age of twenty-one. Clearly, I don't have to search far to find where I get my entrepreneurial spirit.

My dad's favorite sayings were, "I'd put my four girls up against four boys any day of the week." Or "Pumpkin, you can do anything you put your mind to." He always made me feel capable, smart, and unstoppable. When, exactly, had I lost this confidence?

As I watched this amazing man deteriorate over the course of his illness, my outlook and attitude shifted. We had countless discussions during those months about the meaning of life and the need to live out our purpose and passion. While I sat with him during doctor's office visits and rested on my parent's deck overlooking his beloved Kentucky Lake, Dad talked about his fifty years in business, building several businesses from the ground up and then selling them, just to start all over again with a new one. He loved what he did and found joy in the building process. These companies included real estate, printing, ceramic tile, cellular, and so many more. Even though I had heard these stories throughout my life, I began seeing their significance in my own journey.

I began looking at my choices and decided to stop living like a sitting duck and take responsibility for where I found myself and for what I wanted my future to look like. I promised myself that my tomorrows would not be a continuation of my anxiety-ridden hang-ups and misconceptions of myself and my life. I was resigned to the fact that I had a long way to go, but I was worth the work it would take, no matter how much time was required.

Not even knowing where to start, I wrote a list of things I liked to do, what I was good at, what made me happy, and what made the time pass quickly while I was doing it. Turns out time actually does fly when we are doing something fun.

Singing, writing, social media, and health were at the top of my list. Singing was a no-go professionally, but it was definitely a gift I could share in my church's praise band. I started with this because it was easy to jump back into doing something I had already done before. Plus, it didn't take away from my stay-home-mom obligations and even added to my sons' joy because they loved seeing their mom on stage singing to them.

Writing was another gift that didn't require anything besides a piece of paper and a pen or a computer. Within a few months of my dad's death, I started my Christian blog, GEM - God's Encouragement by Meg, where I wrote about real-life experiences, problems, worries, and how to navigate the world we live in. Simultaneously, I began writing a collection of children's books, poems, and songs. I gradually began feeling stronger, and at the end of the day, after a few hours of writing, I felt a sense of accomplishment.

As my spirits rose, one issue remained...I wasn't making a dime. Since I placed such a high value on being an income-producing member of our household, I took my third skill of social media, along with blogging, and offered my services to local realtors who didn't have time or the expertise to provide their businesses with a social media platform face. Being a remote business allowed me to continue to be present and active in my boys' lives, help them with homework, attend school functions, cart them to sports practices, as well as perform the multitude of mom obligations. This business venture lasted for five years, which was a record in my professional life. It sustained my need to be at home with my children and make a little side cash while doing something I enjoyed immensely.

As much as I loved writing, my old friend, "need to make more money," reared his ugly head and convinced me the only way I would be able to accomplish this was by working for someone else. Bad decision. Have you learned nothing, Meg?

Once again, I dove headfirst into the choppy waters.

This period of my life, jumping from one career to the next, was where I beat myself up over and over again because when I reviewed the list of jobs I attempted, I saw a lack of longevity and a waste of time.

The four years of start, stop, and start again with a new position at some company that might be my newfound passion and purpose brought with them an extra twenty-five pounds of baggage by way of my hips and butt. I was forty-seven, heavier than I'd ever been, and currently residing in the deepest depression I had ever been in. And I have been in a few of those pits.

However, this is where it gets interesting. Remember that stint as a productivity coach at the beginning of the four years of playing hot potato? This is where I met Paige, who would later change my life in unimaginable ways. Paige had been a new real estate agent at the company where I worked as a productivity coach, and we became fast friends. I guided her through the process of getting started, the ins and outs of contracts, negotiations, and marketing best practices.

Three and a half years later, I reached out to Paige for her coaching expertise. Since the time we had worked together, she had become a health coach, and I was undeniably in need of being healthier.

I quickly jumped on her health program, lost the extra weight I was carrying on my small frame, and worked to change the leading bad habits that were not serving me well. The great thing is that as I reworked my mindset, my outlook on life transformed. This transformation included what I ate and drank, what I watched and listened to, who I hung around with, and how I talked to myself.

Instead of focusing on all my negative traits, I began to concentrate on my positive attributes and, more importantly, the characteristics I wanted to have. I started telling myself I was worthy, intelligent, safe, courageous, resilient, confident, creative, brave, kind, and grateful.

As I can attest, affirmations are life-giving and life-changing. The habit of affirming ourselves daily may sound silly, and we may not actually believe what we are saying in the beginning, but when things are said over and over, they tend to stick. My favorite affirmation exercise that I still do today is to stand in front of the mirror, look into my eyes, and tell myself that I love ME.

With each baby step, my heart and soul began to mend themselves, and in turn, produced more contentment and peace with where I was and who I was. As I learned to love myself and care for myself from the inside out, I realized that even though my journey had been bumpy, it was absolutely necessary for me to go through it.

What if I hadn't met Paige at one of the many line-item jobs on my resume? I wouldn't have changed my health, and I sure wouldn't have taken the leap to become a health coach, as well. Now, I am able to do all of the things I listed so long ago while staying at home with my boys, who are now in high school, and I make a great living doing it! I get to write, do social media, learn, and teach healthy habits, and I can sing while doing it if I so choose!!

Now I know that success is whatever I decide it is. For me, it isn't about having a cool career, a big bank account, or a huge number of social media followers. It's about looking in the mirror and loving the person staring back at me. I'm happy to say that I finally like who I see.

MEG HAYS

A Texan by way of the Windy City and small-town Tennessee, Meg Hays has always loved using her gift of gab and the written word to encourage others.

With her deep-rooted entrepreneurial spirit, Meg developed and ran several successful small businesses throughout her thirty-year career and is a published author of a Christian children's book.

She currently helps her clients on their health journeys and supports other health coaches in reaching their business goals.

After several years of yearning and looking for ways to live a life of purpose and passion, Meg has finally realized her journey is her own and doesn't have to be like everyone else's. She has found the grace and peace she's always longed for by using her God-given gifts and talents to help others.

https://www.linkedin.com/in/meg-morgan-hays/
https://www.facebook.com/meg.hays/
https://www.instagram.com/meghays72/
https://www.meghays.com

6

EVERYTHING SHAPES US

NATASHA ZIKE

I was born an only child to a mother who didn't want me and a father whose name I never knew. When my mom tried to sell me for $500 in the next county over at two months old, her parents decided to take me in. Since my mom either didn't know or wouldn't say who my dad was, the law wouldn't allow them to legally adopt me and give me the Wilson name, but they took guardianship of me and raised me as their own.

My grandmother had been a nurse, and Papaw served twenty years in the US Army, touring in Vietnam as a chef and living in Germany and Fort Knox, Kentucky. We lived with all the spoils of a retired veteran's life, meaning we lived well below the poverty line. Papaw taught me life lessons like how to change a tire, how to dig cans out of a dumpster—also where I got my first computer—and the value of recycling. Besides military pension and Medicare, this was our only income until I started working at age sixteen.

We lived in a trailer home on a dirt road with a back forty and a garden with about fifty broken lawnmowers of all kinds. I remember my nighttime bathroom as a kindergartner was an empty metal Folgers can, and I tried my damnedest not to cut myself on the jagged edges in the dark. One time, we had a possum get in the house under the kitchen sink, and Papaw caught it in a bag of cat food and drove him out to the nearby lake to set it free. We had a simple life, and our home had a lot of love.

Looking back on my life, a major theme that emerges is loss. Death has shaped me and made me who I am. Losing all the people who raised me starting at a young age taught me to be more present and aware of the fragility of our lives and to see each day and each moment as precious.

When I was three years old, my mom got a second chance to raise me, and I moved to Colorado with her and my new stepdad, Bill, a World War II veteran who I knew as my dad at the time. My favorite memory with them was swinging between their arms in the parking lot, singing a happy chant: "one for the money, two for the show, three to get ready, and four...to...goooo!" as they swung me in the air between them. I do this today with my own three-year-old as much as I can, in hopes that she'll have this same happy memory one day with me.

A year later, they taught me our address and how to call emergency services by dialing 911. We would practice often, and just as I got the hang of it, my mom suddenly dropped to the ground at home and yelled for me to call 911. I did, and the ambulance took her away. Thankfully, she was okay, but it was a frightening experience. Exactly one week later, I was home with my dad, and he fainted. I called 911 again, and they took him away. He wasn't as lucky. The details after are blurry, but I remember seeing him in the hospital bed and my mother and I crying for ages on a bench. He had suffered a heart attack; they buried him at Fort Logan National Cemetery, and he was my first loss. It affected my entire childhood and has been a constant reminder to me that life is short.

"Do anything, but let it produce joy."

—Walt Whitman

My grandparents drove to Colorado, packed Mom and me up, and I rode with Papaw in his beat-up Datsun station wagon all the way back to Abilene, Texas, to live with them again. As we drove, I remember watching the pavement underneath us through the holes in the worn rubber of the gear shift. Three flies joined us for the trip, and Papaw gave them names. He did his best to make the experience fun, and it was memorable, even in the sadness of the situation.

I quickly became Papaw's girl, much like "daddy's girl," and we were inseparable. He took me along for just about anything he did. Since he was retired from the Army, we didn't have much, but he realized he could make some money from recycling cans at the recycling center, so we'd go from dumpster to dumpster, reaching in with an extended metal coat hanger to find and extract our haul. I remember we'd turn in three trash bags of crushed cans for about $100, and afterward, I learned the usefulness of orange soap with grit to clean the toughest grime from my hands. Funny how much more careful I am about germs these days than I was back then. In our back forty, he tended to a large garden he built himself. I remember riding in a wagon behind his riding lawn mower, having the time of my five-year-old life.

Even though we were not blessed financially, my grandparents provided me opportunities to grow and explore my own interests... and get out of the house! They enrolled me in the Head Start program for pre-k, and I think that kickstarted my love of learning and my desire to excel in academics. By kindergarten, I had qualified for the gifted and talented program and rode that until high school. They enrolled me in after-school Spanish, Awanas, Girl Scouts, and the traveling Classical Youth Chorus in elementary school and encouraged me to take up band, tennis, choir, newspaper, theater, and yearbook as I grew older. I even scored a perfect score on a state-mandated TAAS test, and by the time I got to high school, I easily graduated in the top 10% of my class. I was driven to succeed.

When I was seven, my mom married my new stepdad, Jackie. They lived across town. He drove an eighteen-wheeler, and I spent many summers driving around the country, gaining a love for travel with him and my mom. She and I grew closer.

When I was eight, we moved out of the trailer park into a three-bedroom house, my "home," where I spent the rest of my childhood. It was here that Papaw was diagnosed with Alzheimer's disease, and within eight months, he was quickly at the end.

He spent about a week in the hospital, and my grandma's best friend, Debbie, stayed at our house to watch me. We had an eighteen-year-old Chihuahua, and while Papaw was in the hospital, I felt a lump on her. Debbie took us to the vet, who told us that the cancer I had discovered was too advanced. They put her down within minutes. Her loss and Papaw's condition felt overwhelming, like everything was changing too fast—as if everything I loved was leaving me so quickly. It was an emotional roller coaster. At the end of that week, Papaw came home to hospice. His mind had forgotten how to swallow—what a terrible thing to happen! You can't eat or drink. You die by starving to death. My family made the tough decision to allow him to go on his own instead of a few painful weeks with a feeding tube and the same outcome. I was eleven and certain that I didn't want to live without him. I told him and anyone who would listen that he wasn't allowed to die. I lost my dog; I wasn't going to lose him as well. However, the roller coaster was shifting, and something in me started to change.

Late one night, when it was my Uncle David's turn to watch him, I asked to visit. I held Papaw's hand for a long time as we sat in silence. He knowingly squeezed my hand. I told him I loved him and that I would be okay...even without him. Gulp. I told him it was okay for him to go. He died just a couple of hours later. I somehow survived.

"Fake it, 'til you make it. Put on a smile, even if you're sad until you feel happy again."

70

—Mr. Mims, my 6th-grade social studies teacher.

After Papaw passed, Uncle David sort of took his place in my life. He was my *favorite*. He was in the sheet metal business, and even though he lived hours away, he would occasionally visit to repair something and give Grandma and me a little money. I loved him dearly. He would say to me, "Are you ready to go?" "Go where?" I'd say. "Are you ready to go?" he would repeat, and this would continue until I finally said, "Yes," and he'd take me to the park. We had so much fun running around together, up and down the slides, being silly together.

My grandmother, who had never had a driver's license or worked once she married at nineteen, now took on raising an eleven-year-old all by herself. She learned how to drive and survive with government assistance. I knew we needed money, and when I was old enough to start working at sixteen, I got my first job at Taco Bell. I worked there for a year and a half with my best friend. In my junior year, I found a second job as a morning show board operator on a classic rock radio station. By my senior year, a fellow DJ and I were interested in TV news, and we decided to apply to KTAB-TV, the most popular TV station in town. My goodness, we both got the jobs! I quit Taco Bell but kept working at the radio station in the morning and the TV news station at night, with high school in between.

My senior year was busy! Up at five in the morning, off to work at the radio station from six until ten a.m., school until three p.m., then the TV station from five to eleven p.m., all to repeat it the next day! I didn't make a cent above minimum wage, but I had a great time and learned camera work, graphic editing, live television production, commercial design, audio production, and more.

Many others in my life continued to pass, which solidified the lesson that life is short. Death felt constant. Through it all, Grandma was my rock. We became so closely connected as we watched others pass, and we made a point that every time we talked, we showed our love and affection for each other, in case it was our last time together.

We argued about whether or not I would go to college—no one else in our family ever had. The church I attended at the time was a wealthier church in town, and my friends weren't trying to decide *if* they were going to college but *where* they were going to college. She was concerned about how I would pay for it since I would have to cover my own bills and tuition. So, in spite of the full-ride scholarship I had to a school in Dallas, I chose Baylor in Waco due to its smaller TV market, and I thought I'd have a better chance of getting a job there to pay for my bills.

> "Try to learn to breathe deeply, really to taste food when you eat, and when you sleep, really to sleep. Try as much as possible to be wholly alive with all your might, and when you laugh, laugh like hell. And when you get angry, get good and angry. Try to be alive. You will be dead soon enough."
>
> —William Saroyan

Two weeks before I moved to Baylor, I was visiting my boyfriend in another state when I got the call about Uncle David. He had a massive heart attack at work and passed suddenly at forty-three. My entire world shattered—first my dad, then Papaw, now my uncle? My family taught me not to show emotion, but at that moment, I couldn't help falling to the floor, wailing for the world to hear. I had been keeping my grief at bay for years, and at his funeral, I finally let it all out and felt my feelings. This seemed a good tactic to put future grief at bay, and I found that grief didn't sneak up on me on a random Tuesday quite as often as before. I was eighteen, and there were four of us left.

Baylor was a good decision, and I quickly started working at Channel 10 News within a few months of starting my freshman year! However, I needed more money to move out of the dorm. Through networking, I found a job at Dell during my first spring semester. Dell was hard. I worked in a phone-based, inbound queue for consumer sales. I didn't know a thing about the inside of computers, and now I had to sell one to a customer who knew as little as I did! When I started, I had thirty days to learn everything I could, and I learned the value of knowing your resources, including the people around you. I met two bright new hires in my training class who wanted to answer every question I brought them. They saved my job, and we became great friends.

To me, the point of college was to get a good job, and Dell seemed perfect. After my sophomore year, I left Baylor and went to work full-time at Dell in sales. I started when I was nineteen and worked there for almost ten years, eventually moving to their headquarters in Round Rock and progressing through larger and larger sales accounts until I had a forty-million-dollar annual quota in healthcare. I later returned to earn my bachelor's degree in graphic design from IADT, too.

I was twenty-four when my mom and Jackie celebrated their seventeenth wedding anniversary on Valentine's Day. Three days later, he unexpectedly passed a few hours after a standard angiogram while still in the hospital. My mom was devastated. Grandma, my girlfriend, and I went to support her and help with the funeral. There were three of us left.

A year later, on the 6-month dating anniversary with my new boyfriend, we received a call from Grandma saying that Mom had passed away out of nowhere. My mom always had a flair for the dramatic, and I briefly hoped this was a cruel joke. It wasn't, and now there were two.

After Mom passed, Grandma and I clung to each other even more tightly, though we lived hours apart. Two short months later, I got the call that Grandma had a massive stroke. She survived, but she had a long road of recovery ahead of her. My boyfriend, John, and I went to take care of her, and having him by my side during these major moments in my life really solidified him as the steady rock on which I could lean. We married a couple of years later and celebrated our tenth wedding anniversary last year.

Over the next couple of years, we cared for Grandma while she lived at different care facilities. I think it was a way for me to slowly let her go so it did not break me as hard when I finally did lose her. We were always aware each time we met that it could be our last, and eventually, it was. At twenty-eight, the family who raised me was now gone.

> "First, have a definite, clear practical ideal; a goal, an objective. Second, have the necessary means to achieve your ends; wisdom, money, materials, and methods. Third, adjust all your means to that end."
>
> —Aristotle

I eventually took a leap from Dell, trusted my gut, and followed a friend to an unknown start-up with big dreams to "help people see and understand their data." Our Tableau Software office was small and disjointed. Globally, there were only a few hundred employees. The company grew rapidly, had a successful IPO, and our offices moved downtown, occupying one then many floors of an iconic Austin high-rise.

After working there for only three months, I told my boss I wanted to move to London. My grandmother had just passed, and my husband and I didn't yet have kids—a deal I'd struck with him to allow for a few years of travel first. I'd spoken my dreams into existence. I knew what I wanted and aimed everything toward that goal. She said that with my performance, she would help me achieve anything I desired. It became my habit to set a goal, then set another one.

Exactly two years after starting at Tableau, as I turned thirty, I moved to London with my husband and three cats to help spread Tableau culture to their burgeoning office. It was everything I had hoped for and more! We moved into a tiny flat on an inlet of the Thames called St. Saviour's Dock, a block from Tower Bridge, facing Canary Wharf. From my bed or balcony, to contrast the concrete and metal of a bustling major city, I saw the beautiful permanent houseboats filled with such lush greenery. I saw the sixteen-foot change in the level of the river, rising and falling with the tides, filling and emptying the inlet at our flat like an ocean lapping waves on a muddy basin twice a day.

Each workday, I walked two miles along the river from roughly Tower Bridge to the Tate Modern. The scenery was amazing, and I pinched myself as I walked through such historic areas. I left Cinnamon Wharf, which still sometimes smelled of the spice it housed for a century, and walked down my street, Shad Thames, a striking, cozy area in London with its walkways between buildings overhead, under Tower Bridge, seeing the Tower of London across the water.

I'd pass London City Hall, with its seasonal events, and the HMS Belfast, a docked WWII warship-turned-museum, to walk through the Hays Galleria, an old waterfront warehouse-turned-retail center, past London Bridge tube station and London Bridge. I would either pass through Borough Market, a huge food market, or walk by Southwark (pronounced suth-uk) Cathedral and gaze upon the juxtaposition of the 800-year-old Gothic Anglican cathedral with the largest building in Western Europe, The Shard, rising behind.

I'd continue my journey passing the Golden Hinde, Winchester Palace's thirteenth-century remains, and Shakespeare's Globe Theater to see what's on. I'd gaze across the Millennium Bridge, better known as the wibbly-wobbly bridge (a nod to to the good Doctor), or the Harry Potter bridge, and if time allowed, walk through the free Tate Modern to see a Picasso or Van Gogh on my way to the Blue Fin Building where I worked. Each day was something new, some art installation, some new busker, some new event on the water. It was exciting and exhilarating.

London nights were filled with friends at a pub a block from work, where everyone would congregate at the end of each workday. Our office consisted of almost all expats, a multi-cultural melting pot of dozens of languages and nationalities, united for a single cause.

My husband and I started a travel blog and online social presence, TexansTraveling, and each month we committed to visiting somewhere inside the UK and somewhere outside the UK. All I'd ever wanted to do was travel and share photos with those back home. The travel was cheap, and the locations were historic and breathtaking.

We stayed in London for an incredible thirteen months and moved back to Austin to find we were pregnant with our first child! After a year at Rackspace, where I was commuting six hours daily while pregnant, then with a newborn at home, I needed a new job. I wanted to work somewhere I already knew folks. LinkedIn showed me I already knew 120 people at VMware, and they had an open role that sounded perfect! A previous acquaintance from Dell was an interviewer for the role, and even though they had already decided on someone else, I got the job! I built a year-long onboarding program for top-talent new college graduates, and it was one of the best jobs I have ever had.

I trusted my gut again when that same director built a new team of program managers to solve major company issues. I love building things and figuring out challenging problems. It was perfect for me, but leaving a role I loved was scary. I worked as a program manager with her for a couple of years, had our second child, and became a global director, skipping a whole level internally. My mentor said it couldn't be done. I had set a goal and knew it was worth a shot. When I got that role, they offered a 14% pay bump, and I instead negotiated a 36% pay raise, when they typically only offer 3% to 10%, by using publicly available data. I knew what other directors at my company and in my city were getting paid, so I had an expectation, and I didn't waver, though I did have class and tact in how I asked for it.

It's taken me years to figure it out, but I tend to find roles that allow me to tap into my "superpowers" of being a changemaker, being a super-connector—connecting disparate people and ideas, being joyful and inspirational with an edgy and unapologetic but classy style, and being an advocate for the under-represented.

Today I have four official business roles, not counting a few businesses I own with my husband, all of which tap into one or more of those superpowers! They each play a big part in fulfilling my purpose—to educate others, leave this world better than I found it, and lift others up so they can realize their unique potential. My main role is a global product enablement director at VMware, which means I am a "critical connector"—connecting disparate parts of the business with the goal of creating product training for our 40,000 employees, our partners, and our customers on a few of our major product lines. So, with this one, I help lots of people understand our products through the training I create.

In my second role, I'm the global co-lead for the PRIDE@VMware Power of Difference Employee Resource Group (or POD). My global team and I work to create safe spaces where our 1,500 global members and allies thrive and find community while delivering business impact. This role allows me to be an inspirational advocate, and we create programming to train our members and allies in areas of personal and professional development.

Next, I am a member of the VMware PAC with our executives, deciding which US political candidates should receive money from our PAC. I will soon travel to Washington, DC, to meet and host a luncheon for our chosen member of Congress, who represents issues important to my POD.

Lastly, I sit on the Advisory Board of a Texas nonprofit called Texas Women in Business. There are several chapters across the state, and our goal is to create development opportunities for our members, catering to programming that matters to women.

For the past year, I've known a fork in the road is approaching. Normally we see these in hindsight, but I've known significant changes are coming at my company with a major looming acquisition. I've been waiting for all of the paths to reveal themselves before changing course. I will do more speaking engagements; I may also start a consulting business, write more books, or start a podcast—or I may do all of the above! Whatever I do, I know I will keep it focused on my personal purpose, educating and lifting others up along the way, and I will put my full passion behind it and watch it thrive.

Life dealt me certain cards, as life has dealt you yours. We can't change where we started, but we can direct the path we take and own our own narrative. I may have started as an unwanted child in the boonies, but I've grown and spent the last nineteen years in the corporate technology space, working in the US and London, and I am now a global leader at a Fortune 50 company. As I write this, I was just named one of the Top 50 Women Leaders of Austin for 2023 by Women We Admire. Wow!

Through it all, I've learned that everything shapes us. There is life after loss, and knowing life is short helps me be more present now, living a purposeful life where I can choose to be kind and choose joy every day. We can do great things if we focus our minds on a goal (but don't burn ourselves out!). Our social circles and resources will help us achieve more than we ever dreamed, and if we bring our whole selves to the table and step into our own authenticity, anything is possible.

NATASHA ZIKE

Natasha is a passionate LGBTQ+ global leader, speaker, nonprofit advisor, and author whose whole-person, inclusive approach to business creates environments where individuals thrive and business succeeds. She has spent the last nineteen years in the corporate technology space in the US and London and is a global leader at a Fortune 50 software company.

Her empowering messages guide others to live purposefully and joyfully in the face of adversity, making the most of this short life, no matter where they started. She is passionate about diversity, equity, inclusion, and belonging (DEIB) and works to create safe spaces for employees to feel empowered to bring their full, authentic selves to work. In this book, she calls others to lead with empathy, joy, and determination in order to connect with others and find success.

Natasha resides in Austin, Texas, with her husband and two active young children.

https://www.linkedin.com/in/natashazike/
https://www.instagram.com/natashazike/

7

THE GIRL IN THE PHOTO

BETSY R. DAVIS

Upon entering Deb's guest house, I saw a piece of art on the wall that took my breath away...it was me...a photograph she had taken almost twenty-five years prior entitled "Sleeping Beauty." It was thrilling and flattering in so many ways, and it made me nostalgic for the woman I saw. I hardly recognized her in me anymore, but I knew she must be somewhere down deep...serene in her slumber, safeguarding my dreams.

It wasn't just the physical changes that caught me off guard. Sure, I had aged...some of that fiery red hair was now silver. And after carrying and delivering two children as a "geriatric mother," I was seeing myself more like Mrs. Potato Head...oh-so-round, with ever-changing emotion. When I asked Deb's opinion about where that woman had gone, she replied, "I don't know, Betsy. It's like you just got quiet...still lovely and a joy to be around, but you used to own any room you walked into, and now you tiptoe." Her words hit me like a ton of bricks because they were true.

I found myself in this lovely home away from home after being caught by the onslaught of Covid while away on a business trip. Having an "at-risk" husband required an abundance of caution, so what was supposed to be a three-week trip became seven weeks away from him and our two tween boys.

Truth be told, the time away was welcome, despite my misgivings about being away for that long. Somewhere over the course of my twenty-year marriage, I had lost myself. Unhappy for quite some time, it was not a question of whether or not I loved my husband and children; it was that I no longer recognized myself. Seeing that photograph made it clear just how different I had become and triggered an urgency in me to discover how and why.

Objectively, I am an adopted, curly red-headed, Southern, Jewish, freckle-faced, tall woman who has struggled with a weight issue for many years. I am also the youngest of all my cousins, "the baby." By contrast, I was raised in a largely Christian community filled with petite women and friends (with straight brunette or blonde hair), and men who held the power.

Growing up as an outsider...one with plenty of privilege, mind you...I felt like a fish out of water most of the time. I needed to find a way to fit in or make my own place. Like any good Gemini, I did a bit of both. I became a keen observer of what worked and followed suit. I developed a wicked sense of humor, honed the art of shock value, and worked to stay ahead of the crowd and still within the lines so as not to be rejected (again).

Being adopted by my family was akin to winning the lottery. My parents and brother are loving, kind, and generous. Past and present, they are well-loved and respected by many. Appreciation and feeling lucky were ingrained early on, and I treasure this in myself (thanks, Mama and Daddy!). When they came to pick me up, one of the best choices my parents made for us was allowing my nine-year-old brother to sign my adoption papers. He also named me. Even when I drove him crazy as a kid, he looked out for me. We are bonded for life.

My parents defined our life as "comfortable." It was an understatement.

My father worked all the time in the family retail business. It was reportedly started by his grandfather in a tent in Georgia and later turned into a few shoe and clothing stores in Alabama. This business that sustained four generations of our family most likely would have continued to do so had I, or anyone else in my generation, taken an interest. To this day, whenever I visit my hometown, I hear stories about what a wonderful business it was and what fantastic people my grandparents, father, and uncles were...and it has been closed for over thirty-five years.

My mother played bridge at the country club and ran the household. She was lovely and loving and would have preferred a home without a kitchen...just a coffee pot and a refrigerator for leftovers...possibly a toaster oven. When I told her that I was starting a catering business, she asked, "Are you sure you're mine? I cannot imagine anything worse," and we both laughed. I feel her with me almost constantly.

We had full-time help who cooked and cleaned and ironed. They also babysat most nights my parents went out to dinners or dances. Primarily, I had Rachel and Easter in my life, but there were others too. Like most domestic help in the South at that time, they were Black. And if you have ever wondered, *The Help* was real *for the little white children who were brought up by these women.* In fact, it was one of those little girls who wrote the book. Many of the characters, likable and not, were familiar to me.

Rachel and Easter were the seeds for so much good in my life. They are the reason I cook for myself and others. Whether it was Rachel's fried chicken, biscuits, and pound cake (did I mention I'm Southern?) or Easter's cinnamon rolls, their food made me feel cherished and safe...it genuinely felt like a warm hug. That is a powerful skill, and I love passing along that coziness and comfort to family, friends, and clients.

Rachel and Easter offered so much more than just cooking, though. They shaped the way I look at life. They opencd my eyes to a larger world than my sheltered home and exemplified what it was to meet people where they are instead of where you want them to be, and they did it all with love, humor, and dignity.

These women, who cared for us so well and had since my father was a teenager, felt as much like my family as anyone else. Being adopted, I'd already learned that you don't have to share blood to be family. Choosing family (or being chosen) is the foundation my life was built upon. The lessons Rachel and Easter shared, whether intentional or not, made an enormous impression on me. They were outsiders too...*only they could not create the same façade I could to fit in.* They deserve to be celebrated always.

Throughout my life, I have carried many monikers: "the girl who smiles," "the girl who sparkles," "the funny one," "the ballsy one," and "the one who should have her own show." My mother always said, "Betsy goes where angels fear to tread." All were accurate in their moments, and I derived great pleasure from hearing and believing each of them. They represented success to me. They instilled in me a sense of "I'm winning!"

Naturally, something shifted in me when I married my husband and again when I bore each of our children. It was as if some mid-century force had awakened within me that said, "Put them first. You've had your chance." It didn't keep me from having a grand time, far from it! I have had a wonderful life, and I would not take anything for my children...they are the lights of my life. But slowly, slowly, I started believing that voice in my head and postponing my dreams. And then I kind of forgot what my dreams were. Everything was muddled, so I grabbed onto whatever seemed to be the best choice at the time. My dreams became more of a moving target, and if you don't know where you're headed, it's hard to get there.

I straddled the line between being a business owner and a housewife until I felt more like Faye Dunaway in *Chinatown*. *Who was I?* Work became more like a hobby, having just enough success to feel legit but never rising to my ultimate level as I was unwilling to do what I thought of as abandoning my husband and children. Instead, my priority became making a happy life for us all. In and of itself, this is not a terrible choice, but as the years passed, I gave away more and more of myself and my power...to my husband, my children, my clients, and my spiritual community...*everyone who mattered to me.* At the time, it felt like devotion.

I fundamentally believe in making those you love a priority. That was the example my mother set, and it was an amazing way to be raised. Now I realize I can no longer do it to the exclusion of my own hopes and dreams, my own voice.

There is no doubt that the right thing happened to me. *One thing I am clear on is that the right thing happens for all of us.* Our circumstances set us up to learn lessons, and most lessons worth learning aren't easy. They require strength and support. I had so much more of that than I knew at the time. These tests also require honest soul-searching and change. I had to lose my way to find myself again.

My family believed in me. They did not always understand what made me tick, but they supported me in the best way they could. They consistently built me up. Every day, my mother told me, "You can do anything, Betsy, as long as you put your mind to it." She also told me, "You gotta make hay while the sun shines, Darling!" She instilled in me grit and determination. That is how I approached my life as a single person with no children...which is what I was for more than half my life.

I had lots of adventures, dipping my toes into a few careers before that was en vogue. Politics, retail, postgraduate work, and television were just a few. I had quick successes in each field, but it didn't take long to get bored. It wasn't until I found myself in the food industry that I found an itch that needed to be scratched...another awakening of sorts.

People see me as successful, as someone with an enviable life. In fact, I have a charming husband of twenty-three years, two great kids, my own private chef and baking business, meaningful connections with others, and a life filled with travel. It sure looks like success.

At this point, I have to ask myself, "What is success?" Is it always measured by financial gain, professional accolades, or a level of fame? In this climate of "celebrity takes all," I believe everyone is confused. Some days just getting out of bed and delivering the kids to school with breakfast and lunch seems like climbing Kilimanjaro. When I was offered the opportunity to participate in this project, I wondered, "Do I even qualify?"

In my deepest thoughts, I am nowhere near where I should be in any area of my life. That's not a "poor me." It simply illuminates the standards instilled in me as a child. "You can do anything, Betsy...." I am finally realizing that *no one* is supposed to be able to do everything well. We are all part of the whole, and every one of us needs to contribute our own talents so that we all succeed!

What I can say about myself and my work is that I have always wanted to make the world a better place, but I'm seriously not the Peace Corps type. My help comes through love, a large shoulder, and yummy food.

Food is both a great leveler and unifier. It's hard to be in a bad mood with a mouthful of deliciousness. My husband calls me "Pollyanna" for my optimism and distaste for unpleasantness, and I'm good with that. I still believe it really can be as simple as you and your enemy (or frenemy) liking the same thing. If you find your way to one thing in common, maybe you'll find something else, and before you know it, you've found the starting point to a heartfelt conversation...shared humanity as opposed to "other."

The blessing of Covid was the time it gave us all to slow down, appreciate, and reinvent as necessary. For me, that included many changed plans, moving to a new city, and starting over in middle life. I am grateful beyond measure. None of my time was wasted. Everything that came before created what is now...the bad and the good...and ultimately, it is all good.

I'm still searching for my truest calling, and the new and improved version of that woman in the photograph is screaming to take the wheel. Often this is not fun for the ones who are accustomed to the more malleable me, but those who want the best for me are getting on board, and well, those who are not on my team, they can enjoy themselves elsewhere. I wish them well...most of them, anyway.

I'm talented at a variety of things, many of which involve food. My motto for a long time has been, "Food is Love. Food is Nurture. Food is Power." I take joy in feeding people. I understand food's impact on folks, and that excites me. I thrive on good hospitality and know it can change lives and perspectives.

Whether that means I should be cooking, teaching, speaking, writing, or some combination, I have no clear idea right now. As my awakening continues in my new town, I am applying for jobs, taking on corporate clients, and looking to meet folks who need a private chef or bodacious baker in their lives. See? Grit and determination (and no more tiptoeing).

What I hope will come from putting this story out there is real authenticity and healing, not comfortable authenticity, if there even is such a thing. And forgiveness. I'm learning to give myself the same benefit of the doubt I was taught to give others...by my parents, my brother, Rachel and Easter, and many spiritual teachers. Seeing myself with care, compassion, and confidence and being the best *Betsy* I can be, defines success for me.

I try to tell God my plans. Every day, I strive to achieve my purpose...to represent myself and my family well. I stray (a lot) along the way. God laughs compassionately and continues encouraging me to listen more and plan less. Certainty in the process is my new mantra. I wish mercy for you on your own journey. And if you need my skills, please, reach out!

BETSY R. DAVIS

Betsy R. Davis is a private chef, caterer, and bodacious baker. She baked her first cake at eight and planned her first menu at nine. As soon as her father tasted that birthday cake and said, "Thank God for Betsy!" she knew good food and gracious hospitality were keys to unlocking happiness and unity between others. Nothing is as gratifying for her as seeing someone's eyes light up and hearing that almost inaudible gasp when they taste her food.

Born in Alabama, Betsy was a long-time resident of Los Angeles, where she met her husband and founded her company, The Saucy Redhead. Now living in Austin with her husband, Charlie, and their two sons, Elijah and Michael, Betsy is grateful for all life has taught her thus far and feels she is just hitting her stride.

https://www.saucyredhead.com/
https://www.linkedin.com/in/betsy-davis-b66049a/
https://www.facebook.com/BRDavis72
https://www.instagram.com/saucyred/

8

EMBRACING CHANGE

CAROL MEYER

When I was growing up in England, I never would have believed that as a successful career woman and mother of two, I would be living in the US with the love of my life. Before I was seventeen, I was married and the mother of a gorgeous baby girl. This was definitely not in my original life plan, which was to have a successful career and make enough money to travel, buy a nice house, and enjoy life. Getting back on track was a priority.

We worked hard to become a two-career family at a time when most married mothers stayed home. Initially, I worked part-time and then came up with a creative solution: I agreed to pay my mother-in-law to quit her part-time job and take care of our daughter while I worked full-time. Still, by the time I covered that cost, plus my travel expenses and office wardrobe, I was barely breaking even, but I was investing in my future potential.

My job provided me with an excellent opportunity—time off to go to college one workday a week plus evenings—which allowed me to become a fully qualified accountant in five years. There was no time for all the typical fun things of the late teens and early twenties—no going out (except on our birthdays), working multiple jobs, and saving every penny we earned. We purchased our first home when my husband turned twenty-one, which was the legal age for owning property in England. Youthful energy, sheer determination to prove ourselves, support for each other, and our parents' assistance with childcare helped us a lot.

Since I was always good at math, choosing accountancy as a career made sense. A male friend who insisted that his Accounting Institute didn't take women seemed like a challenge I might like to take on. Members of The Chartered Institute of Management Accountants provide professional accounting within companies, everything from cost accounting, budgets, and forecasts to business analytics and strategic plans. To become accredited, you had to pass a series of five stages of exams set by the Institute and have three years of verified experience covering all areas of business accounting. Achieving that experience meant changing companies and even taking some jobs where I was underpaid or overqualified just to get the experience I needed. I worked as a budget officer, financial accountant, controller, and management accountant, as well as in supervisory roles that developed my management skills.

I realized then that opportunities were not always going to be a move up the ladder or to better-paying jobs. I think this was a major catalyst for me in developing new skills, gaining increased exposure, and eventually getting the career that I wanted for myself.

At that time, I was an anomaly—a young married mother in a man's world. There were few women accountants in those days in the UK, let alone one with a family. Once, I attended an interview where, soon after I arrived, I was told that I wouldn't get the job and that they only had me come in because they "just wanted to see what a woman accountant looked like." I persevered, and with my qualifications recently completed, a new home purchased, and the addition of our newborn son to our family, our life felt good.

When my father died at age fifty-five, his death came much sooner than expected, and it brought with it the sudden realization that I had not spent enough time with him. It made me think more about putting "family first." I had taken for granted that the people I love would always be there. Recognizing that I fit the profile of a workaholic, judging success by high pay, a nice home, and vacations, I realized how shallow that felt when compared to being with the people I cared about. My blue-collar parents wanted to see me excel and make the most of the opportunities I had, and I was still trying to prove my worth to them. Making family time a higher priority, I spent as much time as possible with my mother, who lived another seven years after that. I tried to carry this lesson with me throughout my life, always working to make time for those I loved.

In my thirties, I had the opportunity to move into the automotive industry to a position in a different part of the country. The new job was still in finance but focused more managing process improvement, giving me a wider perspective on business operations. The job was interesting, and I was able to move up to a position in the divisional management team, where I ran systems quality assurance (SQA). My role in SQA was very leading edge at the time and was a great opportunity to get exposure through speaking at conferences and writing articles on this new specialty.

The automotive industry, at that time, suffered from a virtually impenetrable glass ceiling, and I was the only woman at my level across all the divisions of my company, The Unipart Group. Soon, the opportunity arose to add the role of the Project Director of TQM (total quality management), which was my first matrix management role with team members in each department.

The divisional head allowed me time to serve on the board of my Accountancy Institute, an international nonprofit organization based in London, which included traveling for meetings on weekday evenings. As the first woman voted onto the board by the membership, I chose the role of chair of PR and marketing, a great opportunity to stretch my wings a little. Who else would give an accountant the role of running a marketing team? I lobbied the Houses of Parliament with other board members and even went to 10 Downing Street, where the prime minister of the UK lives, to network with business leaders and represent the Institute.

I found that taking a proactive approach to nonprofit volunteer roles gave me opportunities to network and broaden my skills and was a great investment of my time.

My next career move was into business transformation consulting with The PA Consulting Group. Because the new job didn't allow time for nonprofit volunteering, I had to give that up. When I left Unipart, many of my female colleagues were sad to see me leave as I had been the most visible woman in that organization. The consulting group had a few more women, though not so many at that time.

I started to take on my own client work when I was the sole employee to volunteer to lead a weekend workshop at a warehouse belonging to a large grocery retailer. The success of this workshop led to more consulting in their other locations and eventually made it a multi-million-dollar account. Being in the right place at the right time and taking the opportunity was the basis of my consulting career.

In the consulting world, typically, you have to sell projects, work at client sites, and demonstrate thought leadership to succeed. My visibility from conference speaking and writing articles led headhunters to present me with opportunities. Connections I'd made at the board level inside large retail organizations made me very attractive to high-tech companies seeking access, alongside industry experience, to help sell their products.

The first of those was NCR, a major player in finance and retail technologies. One thing that I have to thank for that experience is that I met a very special person when a group of technical experts from the US came to teach the European retail specialists about big data and data mining. He was a really nice guy, and we stayed in touch as we both moved on to different companies. Little did I know that, in time, our meeting would be instrumental in completely changing my life.

Oracle then headhunted me into a job as an "intrapreneur" for the retail industry across Europe, the Middle East, and Africa (EMEA).

I was the virtual team leader of about 250 employees who focused on retail across the larger countries in the region, specializing in sales, marketing, product, and services for the countries we worked in.

During this time, I also made some major life changes. As a teenage bride, no one had expected that I would still be married thirty years later. My husband and I had discussed over the years that we had begun to develop different life goals. Things that kept us together had changed, our kids left home and started their own lives, and we had achieved the lifestyles we had aspired to as a young married couple. It was sad to make that final break from my first marriage, but I bought my own house closer to work. It was very feminine, with creamy colors, not suited to the family lifestyle that I had always had before, and I loved it. I felt that it represented exactly who I was at that time of my life.

My job as an intrapreneur was as good as I expected, and I even reported to a female VP in the US for retail. She was my first woman boss. The EMEA management team still had very few women, even in the late '90s! The five years I worked for Oracle were a great opportunity to broaden my experience and use all my skills.

You may be wondering what happened to that special person I met at NCR. He moved to Texas and had a career with Dell in Austin. We kept in touch over the years, and eventually, he invited me to visit him in Austin. A long-distance relationship started to develop, and after several months of travel in each direction, I introduced him to my family. He loved the UK, and my family loved him too, though my daughter did wonder if he was too good to be true. Looking for a job move within Oracle that might bring me to the US so that we could spend more time together, I discovered that my only choices within the company were in California. That was not going to work, so we decided to get married. My husband made a romantic proposal after we chose the ring. I then made what I felt was the only truly emotional decision I've made in my life—I said "yes." No risk analysis,

SWOT assessment, or cost-benefit analysis, and I still have no regrets after twenty-one years.

Discovering that jobs in Austin wouldn't provide the flexibility I needed to travel back to visit my family in the UK, which now included three grandkids, I decided that my next challenge would be to start a business, despite having few contacts and no small business experience.

Not being a high-risk person by nature, I joined the Internet Recruitment Group (IRG), which provided me with systems, training, and a network for a low-cost investment. Long story short, my unforeseen issue was timing—it was 2003, the year of the jobless recovery. Nine months into starting my recruitment business, I did not make a cent in revenue. Even though I had job orders and great candidates, they were never employed. The experience taught me a lot about how to operate a small business, do research, network, and build up my contacts.

Ever felt like a complete failure in your work? This was my low point. Could I make a go of it in the US? I had never before felt such a lack of confidence in my own abilities; it was an alien feeling, and there were waterworks involved at the oddest moments. I knew I had to find a way to get my self-esteem back by being successful at something.

To rebuild my self-confidence, I took a job in car sales for a couple of months at the local Chevrolet dealership. They provided training, guaranteed minimum wage, and flexible working hours. It was close to my home, and the hours allowed me to work on pivoting my LLC toward consulting. Car sales proved to be something I was good at. People liked and trusted me, and being female with an English accent also helped.

During my networking and job search in Austin, I discovered The International Center of Austin (ICA), a nonprofit led by local business owners that facilitate education, business, and culture with an international focus. I interviewed for a job where I had met some of those owners when they were on the interview panel. Though I didn't get the job, I followed up with the executive director of the ICA and became the unpaid VP of business development. I worked pro bono, and he introduced me to everyone in the international field in Austin. I was active in fundraising, planning, and managing large events such as the Consular Ball, as well as conferences and seminars for businesses looking to grow internationally. This also included networking with the local ethnic chambers and cultural groups, and I even hosted an event for some United Nations Ambassadors when they visited. Meeting lots of business owners paved the way for me to get paying consulting engagements with some of them once I made the pivot to strategic marketing consulting work after my car sales job.

I found once again that getting involved with nonprofits was a good way to expand my personal reach, networking with a wide range of people in my new hometown. It was also a good way to make friends.

While my consulting business was doing quite well, I felt constrained in my ability to grow revenue by the fact that I was doing everything. I didn't want to work more hours due to the time I needed for family and travel, so my options were restricted.

I decided to purchase an existing successful business that I could work on rather than in, as an addition to my consulting business. It was much more difficult to find a business before organizations such as BizBuySell were around. It required talking to lots of brokers. Using a franchise consultant who could guide me on which ones could easily be run as a non-operating owner helped me narrow down franchise options.

It seemed that fate was lending a hand when I called FastFrame, a longstanding franchisee of custom framing stores. The local owner in the Westlake community of Austin, Texas, wanted to retire and sell the business. It was six years old, one of the top stores in the country, and in a perfect location. I met the owners, assessed the business, made an offer, and carried out due diligence.

FastFrame fit all the criteria I had set. It was in a great location, with an existing highly qualified and educated staff. The opening hours were very civilized for a retail store, and importantly, there was a low level of inventory with a cash flow positive business model, where clients pay a deposit before you order the materials. The franchisor did not dictate all the processes, leaving me with some autonomy in operations.

However, this was not a low-risk option—it would take a large chunk of my non-retirement savings, and I was unfamiliar with the framing industry. After training, I felt confident that I could grow the business with additional marketing and community engagement, and I began another exciting new phase of my career.

Both businesses flourished. I had retainer clients in my consulting business and was able to grow the store by 20% year after year for three years. When the economic downturn of 2008 came along, consulting was hit first. By 2009, store revenues were impacted. The location had seemed recession-proof, and we did better than most in the industry for that reason. Many frame stores went out of business. Cutting costs where I could, I retained my staff for the recovery. Rent and suppliers were paid on time, and I still made withdrawals. Many loyal clients kept coming back—one of them framed lots of pictures for his garage. An elderly couple came in regularly, and after several pieces were framed, they asked, "How are you doing? We are running out of things to frame but want to be sure you survive."

The systems we had in place captured a lot of client information, sales, and pipeline. In the early days, it was a leading-edge system for the industry, giving me accurate pricing information based on up-to-date purchase costs and the ability to use the data to very effectively manage the business.

Identifying key indicators for the business helped me to ensure profitability, navigate the inevitable economic ups and downs, and avoid running out of funds at a crucial point. I created forecasts of cash flow and expenses to measure against.

After the recession, my challenges changed. Revenue bounced back with marketing efforts, but I lost staff as they moved outside the industry. I found that in a small business, you may have to change your business model a little to best utilize your staff skills. For example, I had a lot of picture-hanging business, but when the person who provided this service for our customers moved on, I had to find a contractor to do this work as the replacement didn't do picture-hanging. Small business owners need to be more pragmatic than leaders in a corporation where there are more people and the roles are more clearly defined.

The store continued to be successful through my fifteen years of ownership. My single biggest month of revenue came from an email that was sent out to several local frame stores. It requested that we provide a proposal for 150 memory boxes with very specific requirements for completion in six weeks and in secret. A nondisclosure agreement (NDA) was required for the project. Of course, I wondered if it was a scam, but I responded to the email requesting the NDA paperwork.

We got the job, at full retail price. In fact, we had been the only frame store to respond. Possibly my fellow frame store owners were unfamiliar with NDAs or thought it was a scam. Maybe they didn't think they could complete it on time as it was a big job for a small store. Having discussed it with my team, covering the secrecy requirement and the need for overtime to complete it, I moved forward with the agreement. Of course, my staff got a big bonus as well as overtime. When they found out which Grammy-winning artist was involved, they were also very excited and proud, but we didn't ever break their confidence.

An exit strategy is a key issue for small businesses, especially in retail. The need to balance revenue growth, a good economy, time left on your lease, and transferability is crucial. As a franchisee, it's important to consider the time left on the franchise agreement and the franchisor's willingness to transfer it. I had a few possible exit points but had chosen not to move on them.

In 2019, it was time, as I was traveling a lot and not focused as much on new opportunities for the store as I had been. While it did well, I knew that it could do better. The business deserved an owner with the energy and enthusiasm I had once brought to it. Selling through BizBuySell worked very well, as it led to multiple offers. Completion took a while as my chosen buyer used an SBA loan, and that required more time than a cash buyer.

Selling your small business requires planning. You need to get your accounts in order and ensure that your processes are well-defined and that there are opportunities for the new owner to develop.

During the time I owned the store, most of my networking was in the Westlake Chamber of Commerce, where I was on the board. Texas Women in Business was also a good group to be involved with. Involvement in the networking groups I joined ensured that I created a deeper level of relationships with other business owners.

Nonprofit activities have always given me a huge amount of satisfaction, as well as the educational and business benefits I gained. Several years ago, I joined SCORE as a mentor. SCORE provides free mentoring for small businesses, workshops, and events both locally and nationally. After I sold the store, I became more involved and am now the chapter co-chair in the Austin area. If you are interested in free business support, I would highly recommend signing up for these free services through www.score.org.

My newest transition is becoming an author, with this project as my first step.

I feel lucky and blessed to have had such a great career that enabled me to live my best life. As I got older, I transitioned to a much more balanced lifestyle that has allowed me to enjoy my life with my wonderful husband and continually growing blended family, my friends, colleagues, and, of course, lots of travel. The person I have become is someone that I would like to be friends with.

CAROL MEYER

Carol Meyer became an entrepreneur in 2002 in Austin, Texas, after a corporate career in Europe, spanning accounting, business transformation consultancy, and high-tech business development with global companies. Embracing change was always a key element of her corporate career, and starting out as a new entrepreneur in a new country was an interesting challenge. Carol has always sought ways to give back and has been very active in nonprofits, both in the UK and Austin. Supporting other women business owners, the small business community, and children's charities have been key elements of her philanthropic involvement in Texas.

Carol's entrepreneurial journey includes consulting, services, retail, and travel. It includes one "failure," the purchase and sale of an existing successful business as well as start-ups. Carol is also currently chair of the Austin chapter of SCORE, providing mentoring, workshops, and events for clients in the Greater Austin area while also supporting and leading the team.

https://www.facebook.com/travelwithcarolatx
https://www.instagram.com/travelwithcarol.atx/
https://www.linkedin.com/in/carol-meyer-84985/

9
ONE FOOT IN FRONT OF THE OTHER

MEGAN MANN

It was December 2021 and a week before college graduation day. I was sitting in bed trying to study for my Spanish final while I had the flu and strep throat at the same time. On the day of my test, my whole family was sitting on pins and needles, crossing their fingers in hopes that they would see me walk across that stage on Saturday.

With shaky hands, I clicked submit. I immediately emailed my teacher and asked if I could have my results before she released them to the rest of the class. My score determined more than just a pass or fail—it decided whether I would finally move on from the tumultuous journey that some people call school. At that point, I began biting my nails and pacing back and forth. I prayed that the extra hours I had put in studying negated the brain fog from my 101-degree fever and the feeling of pure exhaustion.

As I sat there in the same stained sweatshirt and checkered pajama pants I'd been wearing for the past week, I heard the ding of my email. "Megan, Congratulations! You have passed my class. Good luck with your future endeavors." I instantly burst into tears and called my dad. He screamed profanity that I had never heard him use before out of both excitement and relief. We cried together. Instead of hanging my diploma on the wall, I told him I would be putting this email in a frame for everyone to see.

Saturday morning rolled around, and a joyfulness filled the air as I stepped *one foot in front of the other* across the blue and orange platform of Auburn University. I accepted this significant piece of paper I had worked for almost five years to claim. I saw my friends and family in the crowd and offered a glance of "we did it!" and the biggest smile they had seen from me in years.

Ever since I was a little girl wearing my zebra print converse, I never liked school. I know a lot of kids claim that they don't, but for me, it was like a never-ending battle of people older than me telling me that I wasn't good enough. I hated being ranked based on how well I could factor a math equation or if I knew how many bones were in the human body. I hated being defined by a number or a letter grade. Huntsville, Alabama, my hometown, was one of those places that was just large enough that you might see a new face on your last day of school, but it was still somehow small enough that everyone knew your business. I spent most of my time there in an "I don't belong here" state of mind.

The only teacher I had throughout grade school who I felt understood me was my first- and second-grade teacher, Mrs. Childers. To this day, I remember how kind she was. She spoke life into a chubby little girl who had no confidence. She saw something in me that none of my other teachers did for the rest of the years to follow, from third grade to the moment I accepted my diploma. Mrs. Childers was the hope I held onto when I would fall into thoughts of "I am not good enough. I am stupid. I will never be as smart as everyone else here." That just goes to show how impactful and uplifting words can be.

With the help of my parents, I would make it through the many years of school that lay ahead of me. My dad and I spent many nights sitting in the kitchen of the house we had built on our worn-out stools deciphering math problems and finishing science projects. *One foot in front of the other,* I thought. Just *one foot in front of the other,* and eventually, school will be a distant memory.

My parents were always patient with me. I was not the easiest child to raise as I was born with a curious mind that liked to explore everything unknown. I always put up a fight when it came to rules. I was naturally rebellious. I still am. Yet, my parents always knew exactly what to say, how to properly punish my behavior, and when to show grace. I have them to thank for allowing me to be myself in a world that was screaming, "You don't fit in," and for that, I am eternally grateful.

I looked at my mom and dad as superheroes. I didn't realize the weight of the world they held on their shoulders and that they were doing everything in their power to keep it together just for my siblings and me. It was not until 2016, when a tragedy struck our lives, that I saw them for who they truly are. *Human.*

When I entered high school, I discovered a phenomenon that I was not privy to in my years prior. Boys. By my sophomore year, I was head over heels in love with a tall and slender blonde boy who was two grades above me. We will call him C.

C was my first real interaction with romantic love. C and I would skip classes together and drive around in his blue Honda Civic with no cares in the world. We built a friendship that turned into a relationship. It was full of ups and downs as we were just two kids figuring out life, love, and who we wanted to be in this big world full of opportunities.

My memories with him are still some of the best ones that cross my mind. I will never forget the night we sat in his car in a fast-food parking lot and argued about what the future had in store. He was worried that when I went off to college, I'd forget about him. I was certain that was impossible. We cried and held each other, distraught by the idea of living four hours apart. We reminisced about our memories, not knowing that we only had a few of them left to make. I can still feel the love from that moment.

On June 3, 2016, everything changed.

I woke up early that morning wrapped in my purple and blue comforter. I rolled over to check my phone and realized it lacked my usual "goodnight" text from C. I called him a few times, and when I did not receive an answer, I began to worry. The relationship between his mom and me was not the best, but I was desperate, so I gave her a ring. She answered the phone, and her voice quivered, "Come to the house," was all she said. I hung up without asking a question. I remember this drive like it happened yesterday. Ideas flooded through my mind—I was thinking the worst. Tears streamed down my cheeks, and my hands shook as I tried to grip the steering wheel tighter.

I walked up the steps of their house, just *one foot in front of the other*.

The moments to follow would change not only my life but my friends' and families' lives forever.

C had passed away.

That night, I wrote a poem. It was the only way I knew how to let out the grief that encompassed my entire body.

My breath was knocked out at the sound of her voice
Gasping for air
A lifeless body
I was so unaware
What am I going to do?
This can't be real
Physical pain
Hands shaking
Scattered brain
Stomach twisting into knots
"But we were together yesterday?!?!"
Racing thoughts

And as more people walked through the door
One by one knees fell to the floor
Despair
Confusion
What happens now?
I can't go on.

I was a shell of a human for the next few years. I no longer had the strength to perform minuscule tasks on a day-to-day basis. Brushing my teeth and washing my face might as well have been the equivalent of running a marathon or climbing Mt. Everest.

It felt like my life paused the day he died. It felt as if my heart stopped in time, while the rest of the world grew older. I could not understand how the earth could keep spinning without him. It was my senior year, I was supposed to be enjoying all the festivities like the rest of my classmates, but I could not. I missed sixty-four days of school that year. I did not know how to live anymore.

My whole personality was altered as I ached my way through the stages of grief. I will never forget the first time my sadness turned into anger. All of my friends were sitting on the floor of my bedroom with me as I hugged the neck of the stuffed animal C had bought me for Valentine's Day that year. Completely overwhelmed, I began screaming at my best friends to get out of my house. Everyone was so taken aback that one of my friends even left without her shoes. This was one of those eye-opening moments, not just for me but for everyone who loved me. It was a wake-up call that the next few days, months, and years were going to be an uphill battle of nursing my mental state back to a place of normalcy.

We tried. I went to therapy. I got a job. I pretended to be a normal teenager just going through the motions of life. Nothing was working. It felt like I was never going to "get better." I looked to friends and family for help, for any sort of guidance. I am the youngest of three kids, but nobody in my life had ever experienced a loss to this degree. I started to feel hopeless.

For the first time in my life, my parents did not have answers for me. There was nothing they could provide to take away the excruciating pain brought on by grief. As we all struggled, it became more difficult for them to hide their own problems.

I will never forget the first time my mom and I went to eat together, just us, and I realized what was happening. We sat in the dimly lit corner of our favorite restaurant when she asked me what I would think if she and my dad divorced. I could not believe it; so much change had already occurred in my life—I did not know if I could handle more. I wanted to scream and cry and be the biggest baby you have ever seen. But I knew I could not do that. My hands clenched below the table. I took a deep breath, sucked the tears back into my eyes, grabbed her hand, and said, "I will support whatever is best for you both," and we prayed. We will get through this, I thought, just *one foot in front of the other*.

Little did I know that this was only the beginning of four more years of uncertainty, doubt, pain, and struggling to make things work. It would not be until around my twenty-first birthday that they officially decided they did not have any fight left in their marriage. So naturally, to cope with everything I was feeling, I wrote.

> I watched as two people who once said "I do" slowly fell apart.
> Nothing hurt worse than seeing them fall out of love and knowing there was nothing I could do.
> Somewhere in the midst of all the obstacles life had thrown at them
> Their love was snatched away and covered by teary-eyed screams
> Late-night fights and repetitive conversations
> Caught in the middle what could I do
> It was done
> It was too late
> Their love was burnt out
> No matter how hard they tried to reignite the flame

It always backfired and developed into something worse.

The loss I experienced at such a young age brought me mental health disorders that I still battle to this day. I will never forget the first time I sat down at a psychiatrist's office and was "diagnosed" with depression. I remember thinking, "Of course, I'm depressed. I'm seventeen years old and dealing with death and divorce." It did not take a genius (or a psychiatrist, for that matter) to figure out that, yes, I was *deeply* depressed.

This was just the beginning of my up-and-down roller coaster with depression. Little did I know that we would become long-term friends and that I would grow closer to my depressive state than any other. In the next five years that followed and leading into this present moment, depression would become a space so familiar that it almost feels wrong not to have a little bit of sadness seeping through my bones. I think I formed this intimate relationship with depression because, for a long time, I saw that there were two options in front of me—anxiety or depression—and I much preferred the latter. Anxiety makes me feel so unsure—like I need to belong everywhere but cannot. But depression allows me to not care about what other people think—and I was so fixated on whatever I felt depressed about that I could not spare any energy for people-pleasing. Depression felt like a *relief* from anxiety and all other emotions.

My friends and family took on a lot of my emotional baggage as their own. Many people offered their condolences and their shoulders for me to cry on, but my parents, my sister, my cousin Bailey, and my best friend Jane felt the impact of my sadness in ways that I still do not fully understand to this day. They watched me go from a happy girl with stars in her eyes to a ball of depression that exuded hopelessness. My depression bled over into their lives. Nevertheless, they persisted. Each of them made it their mission to help keep me alive, whether that meant forcing me to eat that day or driving me by C's house for the 100th time as I wept.

Depression was another thing to add to my list of trials that I had to "get through" with just *one foot in front of the other*. Things will be okay one day, right?

Writing became my only outlet to cope with the immense amount of pain I felt deep in my soul. Writing was and is a release. Writing lets me work through thoughts that would have sent me down a spiral if they had stayed in my head. When I wrote, I felt less alone, and loneliness was the most difficult piece of my grieving process. Writing allowed me to connect with others in a way that assured me I was not unique in my grief and that other people *could understand* what I was going through. It helped me fall in love with the idea that every human has their own story, and by sharing it, we were all less alone.

This was the beginning of my finding a purpose through my pain. If I had to experience all of this without someone to understand me, then I would make sure that anyone who entered my life from there on out could turn to me when nobody else could comprehend the depth of their pain. Human connection and helping others heal became the one thing that kept me moving, just *one foot in front of the other*.

Writing allowed me to realize that I carried two passions in life: words and people. This is how I decided that I would attend college in pursuit of a journalism degree, with a focus on intercultural communications, combining my two favorite things. This began my journey of "success."

Everyone has a favorite subject: science, math, history, and so on. My favorite subject is people. I love talking to them, listening to them, understanding them, and offering them advice. My family always tells me that I could talk to a brick wall if I wanted to. I have always loved this quality about myself—it is the one thing that comes naturally. It has always been rare for me to be proud of who I am, but once I discovered my dedication to people, I began to flourish.

One foot in front of the other. We are finally getting somewhere.

Something about communicating with others just clicks for me. It does not matter their age, their race, or where they are from, I see every individual I encounter as a soul with a story to tell, and man, do I LOVE hearing stories! Growing up in a small town in the South, there were only a few right ways to do things. As I ventured out of my cooped-up shell, I began to realize that there were many paths to success in life, and nobody else could define what this word meant to me.

As I begin to meet more people, I keep a collection of their stories. I am intrigued by each one. I have a genuine curiosity to learn about as many people as I can. I want to know how they got from point A to point B and everything that came in between. I believe there is a lesson to be learned from every individual, and there is so much to gain from expanding your circle to include people who come from different backgrounds. I believe there is a certain growth that can only come from the knowledge of others.

And I cried tears of joy for the moment I turned left instead
    of right
Where I chose to follow my own road rather than what
    everyone else wanted
I found freedom in my knowledge that my story does not
    have to look like those around me.
For years I questioned why this path was laid out
It feels so uncertain, so not "practical."
But the world needs dreamers, artists, those that are willing
    to express the deepest and darkest parts of their minds
Just as we need people that can mend our physical bodies
We need those that can connect to the loudest voices in our
    heads
There is healing found in the realization that you are not
    alone
That other people feel the way you do.

There's a certain beauty found in reading a piece of work, seeing a photograph, or hearing a tune and thinking, "Wow, that's exactly how I feel."

Writing and humans. This is where I fit in.

~

It was September 2021. I hoped to graduate college in three months. I had no job and no plans for where I was going to live next. I was falling deeply in love—which made it hard to accomplish anything at all—and my family was still navigating how to handle the effects of a broken marriage. At this point, it felt almost impossible that I was going to make it to graduation and walk across that stage. Every day for the next ninety days, I repeated the words just *one foot in front of the other.*

As you all already know, I got the diploma. I made it through what felt like the longest four and a half years of my life. But now it is time to figure out what comes next.

A month after graduation, I picked up my life and moved to Austin, Texas. In true Megan fashion, I did so without ever having visited the city before. Some people might call this irresponsible. Maybe even dumb. I called it spontaneous. To me, it felt *normal.* My sister had moved a couple of months before me, so I had her support waiting on me in what would soon become one of my favorite cities in the world and the place I now call home.

In one year of living in Austin, I have accomplished more than I ever thought I could before the age of twenty-four. I built an entire life from the ground up. I met an incredible group of people who have become a support system for me. I have worked three different jobs, each of which has allowed me to grow in different ways. I have used my skills with people and communication to quickly climb up a ladder that I started at the very bottom of. I have discovered that there is so much life beyond the walls of Alabama and the city I grew up in.

Most importantly, I have realized what success means to me. I have always been someone who appreciates the simple things—the sun shining on my face after a few days of rain or the way someone's eyes light up at an unexpected compliment. Success, in my book, is not having the most money, being the fittest, or even finding a "happily ever after." It is having peace of mind; it is doing whatever I can to leave this world a little better than I found it. After spending so many years in a constant state of distress, the expense of a calm mind is priceless.

I was always so worried that I would never be successful, that I was never going to be good enough. I spent so long hanging on the coattails of all the people around me. I spent my whole childhood looking at small parts of people's lives and confusing them for the whole. I had to learn that success cannot really be viewed from the outside. I see now that success does not have one singular definition. Success is specifically tailored for each individual to mean something different.

I wish I could go back in time and hug the little girl who spent countless hours sitting on her bedroom floor, just hoping that some way, somehow, she could be just like everybody else. I would tell her that she was born to stand out. I would let her know that her journey was going to be difficult yet so incredibly beautiful.

I would tell her that life is not going to be easy, but we will make it through—one day at a time with just *one foot in front of the other*.

MEGAN MANN

Megan was born and raised in Huntsville, Alabama. She graduated from Auburn University with a degree in journalism and moved to Austin in January 2022 with no job and without ever visiting the city. She now works full-time at a job she loves and has more motivation than ever to work toward her goals.

Megan is known as the "free spirit" of her family, as she has typically taken the unconventional path in life. When she was younger, she experienced a loss that changed her world and sparked her relationship with writing. Megan turned her pain into her passion and used writing as an outlet to cope with grief. Writing has not only allowed her to heal on her own, but it has connected her with so many others who have been through similar situations. She realizes that her journey is allowed to look different than everyone else's, and she gets to define what success means to her.

https://www.instagram.com/meganmann_
https://www.instagram.com/whatsleft_unsaid/

10

WHEN THE HEART GETS QUIET

SANDY STEWART

T he art of tap dancing is about saying something. Tap dancers want to learn to tap dance fast because they think that means they've graduated, but if all you make is noise, you end up making white noise. It's like when someone's loud talking, and it ends up being just a dull drone of them saying nothing. A tap dancer's intentional points of well-placed silence can speak volumes.

Silence is not just a moment without sound. It's the space where we breathe, the time we take to do the very thing that makes us truly alive. "Silence holds the most important part of what you want to say." This is a concept paraphrased from tap dancer, choreographer, and dear friend Acia Gray.

In the three years leading up to the pandemic, I was living my life like a stupid-fast-tap-dancing loud-talker. My life was fast and furious. It started with a major life change that I wasn't ready to deal with, so instead, I filled every second of every day with something to do. Not once did I sit down for just five minutes to just take a breath or reflect. I never checked in with myself, never got quiet, and never paid attention to what was going on for me. I was doing everything…work, workouts, live music with friends, tap classes, yoga, volunteer work for three nonprofits...literally everything I could. But I did NOT spend time with myself...until I had to.

And then I spent three years, my "silent" years, rebuilding everything. It took widespread loss to cut through the noise of my business and sinking into silence to rebuild my life. I had lost my business, my mom and a dear friend, many friends who moved away, my health as I knew it, and a place to live...it's hard trying to remember all I lost. My life was gutted, and I was taken down to the studs.

In my early days of being in business for myself twenty years ago, I was working with an Australian-based business coaching company that was setting up in the US after establishing in the UK. For the first year, on a steep learning curve, I thought I was racing to keep up with my cohorts in the UK. Then while attending a training in Richmond, outside of London, a group of them asked me about my clients; how many did I have, how long did I have them, and how did I get them? I was so embarrassed to admit I only had five. My stats were going to show my insecurity with big, bright lights. But they were wowed! They didn't have as many, and the ones they had were handed to them. I had help from my mentor, but I got the leads, got the meetings, and established the relationships on my own. Then, I got to watch my mentor close the sale. Those UK coaches wanted to learn from me about how I was doing it. While I was surprised and honored that they looked to me for advice, I lacked the confidence to believe I had much to offer them.

But there I was, blonde, female, and young...the three qualities that meant, in my mind, I would be dismissed, brushed past, and even ignored. What value could I possibly bring? Having sales meetings regularly with seasoned CEOs, predominantly men, was beyond intimidating. Then, another mentor asked me something that changed my trajectory...did I have just one thing to say, just one thing to teach them? All I needed was one. I didn't need to have the same years of experience or number of awards, but I did have something, one thing that I could share that would help them. That one thing was all I needed to feel some confidence, and that one thing gave me wings.

While knowing I could offer value gave me confidence, it didn't always mean that I was treated fairly or with respect. This showed up for me in business with business partners, of which I've had numerous. There's a lot of ego in the world of white collars, and when a big ego feels threatened, like a dog, it'll growl and show its teeth. Many times, I was dismissed or taken advantage of, I believe, because they felt threatened by me.

It can feel threatening to a CEO who has a whole career behind them and already knows everything for a young female who doesn't look like she's had a hard day in her life to show up with something to say.

I learned it had nothing to do with what I had to say, what I could teach, or what it could do for them. They needed to feel okay that I wouldn't embarrass them or, better yet, that I could make them look good. This built my resilience, and I learned how to exude confidence...down to details like how to enter a room for a sales meeting—walk in like an exclamation point, not a question mark, with enough speed to show relaxed confidence, but not so much that you look cluelessly eager. Pick a commanding seat; it could be the middle of the boardroom table or the end, depending on how many are in the meeting. Immediately locate the highest-ranking person in the room and be the first to introduce yourself to them with a handshake. This is how you fake knowing what the hell you're doing. The only problem is the first time I did it, it worked so well that they looked to me during the meeting to answer the tough, most important questions, and I had no idea how to respond to anything yet. So, then I had to be a quick study on how to answer their questions or respond to their remarks.

I learned not to believe every dog's bark. Most times, they were just trying to be scary, so I'd back off, get distracted, or, best yet, I'd be confused as to why they got all barky in the first place. It's a thin veil of deceit. They were barking because I got too close to some truth they didn't want me to uncover. I learned to stay strong and expect the truth from people. Either they will either give it to me, or their bark will get louder, and the crazy will become more and more obvious.

Typically, if I'm confused about what someone is saying, it's not me; it's them. Sometimes, ego-driven people maintain the upper hand by just being confusing. I had to learn that if I'm confused, it doesn't mean that I can't understand, but there is a potential that they are hiding something. Sometimes, what they're hiding is their own insecurity, and my presence may have felt like a threat to them.

Stay present. Stay inquisitive. Good, solid, honest, caring people of integrity will not mind you asking deeper questions.

Doing the work was never an issue of confidence, but selling the work was. Sure, I had a lot to learn, but I'm a life-long learner, so bring it. After leaving the global business coaching company, I set up shop with my brand new husband in a brand new town. I don't recommend that anyone quit a job, get married, start a business, and move to a new city, all within thirty days, but that's what I did. We started the business together, and his sales skills were sharp. Even at my best, it was still an effort. So, we chose to divide and conquer. He was better at sales and strategically brought me in so I could show heart and validity, and so the client knew who would take care of them. And I did take care of the clients. I also ran our operations, which outside of sales and client work, just felt like it included "everything else."

We took the stage together. We co-presented to clients, then graduated to co-presenting workshops, seminars, speaking engagements, and, finally, our own conferences. We set up a license model to teach others how to do this work and build this kind of business. We grew it to nine offices in five states. In our circles, we were a big deal.

I hated it.

The most enjoyable time for me was when I was onsite at a client's office, on a whiteboard with the owners, and sometimes managers too, strategizing, getting creative, coaching, planning, pivoting, scaling, listening, and counseling. THAT I loved. But every time I left one of those sessions, reality was waiting for me.

I could not escape or handle the stress and pressure of running that business. My husband and I had very different tolerances for risk. On a scale of one to ten, one being "avoids risk at all costs," and ten being "nothing is too risky," I was a three, and he was a ten. Financially put, just add some zeros, and that's how much either of us felt comfortable investing in the business before wanting some kind of payoff.

That's a hard place to find yourself because it meant he had to slow down, and I had to speed up if we were to meet in the middle. The thing is, to me, it sure didn't feel like he slowed anything down. He is someone who has really big energy, which can be intimidating to most. Somehow, he didn't intimidate me in the boardroom, but when it came to talking about our finances, forget it. Most often, when I brought it up, he was pissed off and refused to discuss it. For the times I did successfully say how much we needed to make payroll, he could go and get it. It was some impressive manifestation, magical even. If only we could have been able to discuss finances freely, we would have been a money-making machine. I truly believe that.

Even now, seven years after we split up, it's still embarrassing to admit, but instead, we went from a deep financial hole to just filling the hole, then back to digging another deep financial hole, over and over and over. But we lived so that we appeared to be successful in every way, even though we weren't in almost any way.

He thought we needed to appear to be successful. Otherwise, how could we sell the success we're promising our clients? He needed success like our lungs need oxygen. And whatever success we did or didn't have, he certainly wrapped it up in high-quality, opaque wrapping paper of optics. So we had the house, the cars, all the things as if we were. But we weren't.

Success for me is a feeling of confidence in every aspect of my life, enjoying my work, getting paid what I'm worth, and having enough in my bank account to be able to sleep at night. Leveraging debt to finance business growth can be really smart business, but creating debt on a scale way past your comfort zone only just to fill the hole is not.

Our marriage crumbled once I learned that the façade of success bled into our personal relationship, too. His well-crafted optics were used on me. Nothing was as it seemed. And with the level of stress and pressure our business was, why on earth would I stay in a marriage that offered me nothing?

Being in a business relationship with your romantic partner is doable, but no matter how well you manage it, there's one thing you cannot escape. On the one hand, if there's a win in the business, you both feel it. On the other hand, if there's stress in the business, you both have it. And if it's overwhelming stress, you can't be there objectively for each other. That is just impossible, not objectively, not without having your own feelings too. I couldn't, anyway.

Splitting a business in a divorce is not too dissimilar to splitting custody of kids. The business was our child, but unlike a child, neither of us wanted it. We set up a spinoff company that he ran, and I got the original business. Thanks. I didn't want it at the time, but what else was I going to do? It was all I knew. I tried to make it feel like my own, changing things here and there. But there were way too many ghosts throughout that entire business until, eventually, I just could NOT sell anymore. Deep down, subconsciously, I did not want more clients. I was my own hurdle. My revenue was dropping, and without any new clients on the distant horizon, I was going into debt all over again.

Then, my friend, Lori, posted a meme on Instagram, a quote that said, "One cannot heal in the place they got sick." That idea sunk into my psyche, and two days later, on January 23, 2020, just weeks before the pandemic, extreme burnout and heartache stopped me in my tracks. My path ended in an instant with a huge pit in my stomach and dropped me to my knees. I literally just couldn't go on.

I decided to keep going on all the existing client projects and follow through on all that I had promised people because being true to your word is one of my key values. But I wouldn't try to get anything new until I knew what I was going to do. That was intended to be a twelve-month nice, long, slow ramp down to finish client engagements and figure out what's next. Then, the lockdown halted business for most of those clients, and I lost 85% of my revenue in two weeks.

Letting my key employee go was one of the hardest things I've ever done. She didn't deserve to lose her job, and how could I tell her that I just couldn't keep going? We had things happening, real, hopeful things. This came out of left field for her. Still, to this day, I feel bad for that, for her, for how suddenly and surprisingly it happened. When the road suddenly ends, that's it. It just ends.

I am a survivor, though—of sexual abuse, narcissistic abuse, serious self-doubt, alcohol abuse, thirteen-plus months of houselessness (during a global pandemic, no less), of having to leave my mom in a Covid unit at a hospital to die alone, of grieving the death of my mom all alone in quarantine with just my thoughts, of being tricked into signing an incorrect version of a legal contract that left tens of thousands of dollars on the table that I didn't have, of my own over-reliance on myself, of liars and cheaters, and of egos the size of football fields who tried to take advantage of me because I am a woman. I looked young, I'm blonde (well, blondish silver now), and I came across as small, less than, "not there yet," and naive. I was naive. I was a target.

Or so I thought...

I'm none of those things, actually. It took me a long time to realize there's a vast difference between what people perceive me to be and who I really am.

Now, entering my twenty-second year of working for myself, I'm right back at square one, starting over completely. The business I built to a scale of nine offices across the US and one in Sydney, Australia, certainly looks good on paper, but it never felt like my version of success. Oh, there were some amazing successes. I helped our client businesses get profitable, so they didn't have to cut benefits, salaries, and people. They got efficient; they won best places to work awards; they got profitable; they enjoyed their businesses again; they thrived.

It's taken me some time to get rid of the ghosts so I can accept the wins. When I hit my brick wall and then suddenly lost it all, that level of amputation was a shock to my system. I was already trying to settle into the idea of closing my doors after being defined by it for so long. When lockdown took the rest of what stability I still had, I was unnerved, to say the least. In the middle of hitting a life-altering brick wall and lockdown, one of my closest friends died unexpectedly. Then, weeks later, I put everything in storage and lived out of a suitcase for the next thirteen-plus months.

Originally, my plan was to spend maybe six months house-hopping, seeing friends around the country, and working remotely while I figured out my next step. But with only one client left after lockdown AND a pandemic shutting down interstate travel, that idea dissipated. I moved "home" to my sister's house and was grateful to have landed there so I could help my mom (remotely) while she navigated assisted living and the cancellation of all programming and community dining with a downward spiral of Alzheimer's. Time with my mom replaced half my work day. I will never regret the magic and beauty of being able to show up for her like that, and I could not have done that if I hadn't lost so much business. For all those out there who also showed up for someone in a long-term care facility, I see you. We haven't even met, yet I'm bonded to you for life. That stuff was not easy!

I've heard that trauma is simply dealing with something alone. Taking advantage of slower times, I sought out trauma therapy. That's some life-saving stuff, moving giant boulders out of the way and off my back. The work of angels, for sure. I had never really allowed myself to get angry about the end of my marriage and the business, but trauma therapy held my hand, and so it came. It culminated in me mentally freeing myself of it all. I burned my ex's things in my mind while meditating to the sound of fire. When I confessed this to my therapist, she laughed out loud and said, "Good, keep doing it. And keep doing it until you're bored with it." Ahh, permission to mentally pyro. It was liberating.

As I finally got angry, I also worked through many other deeply recessed treasures I never wanted to look at. It was hard and painful, but I had time, and because I was already so lost, it felt like the only way through. I can never thank my sister and brother-in-law enough for giving me space in their home to work through years of baked-on crud suffocating my heart.

After freeing myself up some, I sought out inspiration for what was next and found a cohort of folks looking for the same in an online program that met twice a week. Through that process, I came to realize that it did not matter what work I was doing. My JOB, if you will, my purpose, was to be so connected to myself in the most authentic and loving way because when I can do that, really do that, my purpose shines through no matter what I'm doing for work. When I connect, I shine, and when I shine, THAT'S when I effortlessly and positively impact those I come in contact with. THAT is my job. Sounds hokey, I know, but honestly, this concept was so clear to me, and the idea of it just seemed alien. It was a moment of aha, so vividly clear and unwavering. It was my burning bush moment. Life-altering.

So…I decided to go back to school. The University of Cambridge Sustainable Leadership Program went virtual, and I began the program with about 240 other students from around the world. Going back to school and writing papers twenty-eight years after graduating college was no small feat. For those who have done it, I salute you.

In the midst of completing these studies, my mom passed away, AND my health tanked unexpectedly, so for the next ten months, my focus was on survival. Debilitating digestive issues and seriously intense brain fog crippled me. I wasn't able to leave my house most days and couldn't make plans with friends without the caveat that I might cancel on the day if I wasn't well, which happened most of the time. "Hidden" illnesses are horrible because, on the outside, you appear fine, but in reality, you are crippled. Ten months without an answer sent me into depression, and I was despondent, believing this would be my life forever. It felt horrifying to accept that I wouldn't be able to socialize again in my life, work again, or even date. How could I do any of those things?

However, I finally found a doctor willing to run tests to find out what was wrong. The answer came: my pancreas had insufficient function. Now, with supplements and a restricted diet, I am able to manage. I may deal with this for the rest of my life, but at least I can now manage to have a life. About five months after the supplements and restricted diet took effect, even my brain fog lifted quickly. I felt like I woke up from a coma. It was instant. Looking around, I realized ALL the things I hadn't been taking care of, including mail that was many months old, but I began. One day at a time. One step at a time.

Even dating became an option, and beyond luck, an amazing guy from my distant past magically appeared and helped me to feel like a human again, attractive again, a woman again, truly valued.

I also regained enough gumption to redefine the work I wanted to do. It's taken some time, but I stuck with it. Now, I have incorporated all the knowledge and experience I gained and added in the component of sustainable leadership for businesses. I have developed an online training platform for managers to develop and run a sustainability function within the company, teaching them high-level strategy so they can think like an owner. I've established a carbon footprinting initiative for companies getting started, performing value growth assessments, operational audits, and sustainability opportunity reports with twelve-month rollout plans.

All of this fits under the umbrella of environmental and social governance (ESG). With over thirty million small businesses in the US, together, we can make a huge impact. I'm teaching and consulting, and finally, it feels 100% mine. This is me, authentically. What's next, I do not know, but I'm game. I'm here for it. And finally, I'm excited again.

So, this is how it can be done, I guess, a complete reinvention of a person. Rip out everything you know, and lose so much that the only thing left to do is start over. I don't recommend forcing utter devastation; rather take full advantage of any loss because inside that gaping hole lies the power to regenerate and rebuild. Before the pandemic hardly had a chance to start, I lost my business, my mojo, a dear friend, and any stability I thought I had. In the midst of the loss of everything, I began to feel more connected to my heart, my family, and nature...and I developed deeper, more meaningful relationships than I ever had. I have so much gratitude for all that has happened and all that I've lost because, without it, my life would not be as absolutely beautiful and hopeful as it is today. I regret absolutely nothing.

After losing what felt like everything, my silent years are now beginning to dance with sound, with vibrancy, and with a whole new rhythm that I could only dream of, including a lot of well-placed silence.

SANDY STEWART

Sandy Stewart is the creator and founder of Think Big, an outsourced sustainability support and training program for small- and mid-sized businesses. Her twenty-two-year career helping SMBs and SMEs grow value now has an added focus on what's known as the triple bottom line (people, planet, and profits). She believes that companies that care for their people, their customers, and their community have a duty to run a profitable, thriving business. When a business shrinks or closes, it negatively impacts all those employed and the customers and community around them.

Today, she's a speaker, trainer, author, social impact strategist, carbon footprint specialist, value growth expert, small business advocate, and board member. Her current volunteer work includes being past president and VP/treasurer for Tapestry Dance and founder and membership chair for NAWBO Austin.

https://www.linkedin.com/in/sandy-stewart-9534a/
https://www.instagram.com/thinkbigprogram/
https://www.thinkbigprogram.com

11
BARRIO GIRL TO BOSS LADY

JANENE NIBLOCK

Hi My name is Janene, and I'm an overachiever. My overachieving started early. I think my mom still has a drawing from third grade where I said I wanted to be a brainy neurosurgeon! Who knows where I got that from? *General Hospital* daytime television, maybe? Competing with my peers to see who could finish our assignments the fastest was a common occurrence. In second grade, I was placed in the gifted and talented program, where I remained for all of elementary school. After high school, I pursued a degree in premed. It was hard, way more challenging than high school, but pushing myself to the edge was my only mode of operation. Little did I know that compulsive tenacity would be the greatest key to my success as well as my greatest downfall.

Growing up as the eldest of seven siblings, it was natural to be the bossy big sister or second mom in the house. We were a middle-class family in Laredo, a border town in Texas. My dad worked for the oil field, and my mom mostly looked after us kiddos. She would help my nana at her optical store part-time. We didn't discuss finances as a family, but I remember my dad getting laid off after my brother Steven (number four!) was born and feeling a lingering stress and tension embarking on the household. We had to move from a private Catholic school to public school, subtle indicators of cost savings, and figuring things out. We never went without, but I wanted to have money to buy myself cool clothes, makeup, books, and things that I enjoyed.

My parents were uber laid back, which fostered a self-starter mentality. They loved us unconditionally and never pushed us to do anything we didn't want to. At sixteen, I started my first job working at a tutoring center. With such a large family, I felt a responsibility to help my parents and contribute to the household, making me even more determined to make something of myself.

During my sophomore year at Texas A&M International University in Laredo, two of my best friends convinced me to move with them to Austin, Texas, and transfer to the University of Texas at Austin. We were all accepted, and I ventured out of Laredo into the big wide world—or at least that's how it felt. Once I arrived in Austin, I had my own room for the first time in my life. I had space, I could breathe, and I was exposed to a whole new way of life. It was exhilarating, scary, and grown-up—a huge contrast to my house of ten (my youngest sister, Kelly, was only two years old when I moved out of the family house). Ahhh, no more diaper changes or feeding my baby sister. I missed my family terribly, but at twenty-one, I felt like I was in the right place with only myself to look after for a change. I worked part-time at the HEB, a local grocery store that was walking distance from my apartment and took the bus to campus.

It was the weekend of my birthday, February 28, and I made a trip to Laredo to celebrate with the family. Saturday morning, my mom woke me up and said that my roommates had called me to tell me that our apartment burned down. There were about six units that were affected, and our place was toast. I lost nearly everything. This experience turned my world upside down. The apartment complex we were in found a sister complex that had availability, but it was much farther from campus and work. We were fortunate that the Salvation Army could donate furniture. I didn't have renter's insurance, but my parent's homeowners insurance kicked in a little bit for out-of-home loss contents. Fortunately, no one was hurt or injured, and I was able to salvage a few photo albums and books.

My new commute was longer, and I was feeling extremely unsettled. I failed botany and was failing calculus, and combined with my already wavering commitment to premed, I was anxious to graduate. After taking a semester off to get back on my feet, I met with a career counselor and decided to switch to a psychology degree. Many of my classes would still count toward psych, and I had a natural affinity for helping people. As a therapist, I could still help folks navigate the challenges of life even if it wasn't in a hospital setting or doctor's office. Plus, hello, I was in my early twenties in one of the most vibrant college towns; I wanted to have some fun.

Cue tech job. I was offered a telemarketing role at a software company called Vignette, making twice as much money as I was making at HEB. It was part-time, so I could work and keep up with my classes. Companies during the late '90s invested a lot of money in their employees. They fed us, we partied, and there were a lot of perks. I wasn't prepared for what was to come when it all went belly up in the 2000s. My boss called me to a meeting with HR where I learned that I was being made redundant, and they needed to review my severance package with me. It was shocking and I cried, unsure of how to manage this unplanned occurrence. There was a group of us who had all been let go and were being escorted from the building with our boxes. We went to a bar afterwards to debrief and talk about what to do next. I had bills to pay, and this wasn't part of my plan. I started claiming unemployment and searching for a new job. Wait for it…

A *week* later they called me back offering me my old role as a contractor. I could double-dip, a severance package still in place and get paid an increased hourly wage. No more tears here! After a few years as a telemarketer, I was promoted to the database marketing team, which I loved. I didn't want to go down the sales path because I hated rejection. However, I loved cleaning data, researching demographics, running reports, and sending out email communications. Eventually, I moved into a business analyst role liaising with the IT team on how to improve our customer relationship management system. I also ran new hire training sessions for our sales team. During the remainder of my time at Vignette, I survived fifteen rounds of layoffs, desensitizing me to the ups and downs of the corporate world. These experiences taught me how to read the signs of company changes and restructures so I wouldn't be surprised. I always had plans B and C and made it a point to start saving money.

About a year after I graduated from UT, I decided to pursue my degree in counseling. I enrolled in the master of arts counseling program at St. Edward's University, taking evening classes part-time. Working full-time just wasn't enough for me, I always had to strive for something more. It took me about five years to graduate, but I did it. Still, with an appetite for helping people, my plan was to become a licensed professional counselor. Being a great listener, people still naturally gravitated toward me for advice and mentoring.

Meeting my future husband was one of the most significant outcomes of working for Vignette. Simon was based in the Australia office and had come to Austin for a sales boot camp. We sat across from each other during dinner. I thought he was married, and I was engaged at the time.

Having doubts about getting married was so stressful; it was the first time I started to have health issues. Because guess what, if you don't work through your emotional shit, then it will present itself physically. Feeling overwhelmed and anxious about this major life commitment led me to see a therapist. My parents were so amazing, they never fought. I think they forged an alliance to survive raising seven kiddos. This made me grow up thinking everyone just got along, and I was a bit naive about confronting conflict. So, I lacked some major coping skills and didn't want to burden anyone with this decision of "to marry or not to marry." Since meeting Simon at dinner and working together on the same team even though we were in different offices, we kept in touch. He visited a few more times that year, and I realized that we had a very special connection.

Needless to say, I called off the wedding, and using my honeymoon travel credits, I flew to Australia for vacation a few months later to visit Simon. After a nine-month long-distance relationship with both of us flying back and forth for visits, I decided to move to Sydney. Oh, he was divorced by the way and had two adorable boys. The border town girl was moving to Sydney. Here we go!

Even though I had just graduated with my master's in counseling, I decided not to get certified since I was moving to Australia. I figured I could go down the counseling route in Sydney once I got settled. It turned out that accreditation was not the same in Australia, and I would have had to go back to school. Since I was doing so great in the tech world, I decided to stay put.

When I talk about moving to Australia and getting hired by one of the top consulting firms that also sponsored my work visa, I often say I was lucky. But that is a misnomer I find so many of us make. It wasn't luck. I worked my ass off, and I was smart and had amazing experience in database marketing and technology. I've learned after all these years to own my worth. Through a seven-year journey in therapy, I built a huge toolkit of skills and learned the importance of self-love.

Moving across the globe was a big transition. I left my friends, my huge amazing, adoring, loving, supportive family. We did not have WhatsApp or free WiFi calls at that time. It was expensive to make overseas phone calls. We weren't as experienced using Skype and there was no FaceTime. It was hard; I missed my people. But, boy, I loved this guy, and his boys and I persevered. It really made me toughen up as an individual. Australian companies love hard-working Americans with their ridiculously dedicated work ethic. I was a superstar there, earning lots of money. I was mentored by incredibly smart leaders, who empowered me to grow professionally and personally. I was introduced to what is called a "High

Performing Values-Based" organization and "7 Habits of Highly Effective People" training. Don't forget—massive overachiever here!

At one point, though, I decided to take a break from the tech industry to make the transition to counseling, still having an untapped yearning to help others in a professional capacity as a therapist. Maybe I was trying to figure out what my true calling was. Plus, since I had invested so much time, effort, and money into studying psychology and counseling, I felt like it would be a waste if I didn't follow through. I quit my job and tried to do some volunteer work with a few nonprofit organizations. But it just wasn't working. Everything felt like an uphill battle. The commute was too long, the pay wasn't enough, or I felt like I was going backward. I decided to start my own company doing project management and Salesforce consulting. I discovered I did not like to acquire leads and sell my skills. I had a few contract roles, but it wasn't enough, and I lacked a sufficient business network in Sydney to make it work.

One of my former managers called me and said he had a role for me with an out-of-home advertising company in sales operations. I decided to go for it, and I'm glad I did. I was in a new industry and again soaked up the brilliance of everyone around me. I thrived in Australia, but big city living is hard, and the boys grew up, and we needed more space. Simon wanted to transition from high-tech sales to counseling, so we made the decision to move to Austin, Texas.

It was serendipitous to have the opportunity to move with Eye Corp to the Austin office. You know things are meant to be when the universe conspires to make things easy. Of course, it wasn't easy leaving the boys with their mum, but it was a decision we felt was right for us at the time. Simon was able to study full-time to get his master's in counseling, and I was the primary breadwinner. We bought a house and settled in, reestablishing friendships and family ties, and making new friends, too.

I became unhappy in my job (again); the out-of-home advertising industry wasn't doing well and the company was shrinking. I was running business systems and IT, which was awesome, and I had learned a lot, but I had reached a ceiling in terms of what I could accomplish in the role and with the company. Plus, I felt trapped because I wanted to support my husband's goals but at the same time I started resenting being the only one contributing to the household. I was tired of holding down the fort. Marriage is hard, but he finally said, "Just quit, we'll figure it out," so I did. I spent a few months in London, helping one of my best friends with his company, and when I came back, I landed a new role as director of sales and marketing for a supply chain software company. It felt so great to get a fresh start. My boss was amazing. I was again surrounded by super smart and supportive colleagues. The company went into high-growth mode and began acquiring other companies.

And what happens with overachievers? We get assigned all the projects; "Give it to Janene," they would say, "she'll get it done." Of course, I loved this because I was the superhero. And I love people. I wanted them to like me and praise me. But let me tell you, it took a toll.

I was forty. I had been at this type of work for a long time. Companies in growth mode will take everything you will allow them to. And I didn't know how to say no. It was subtle at first. I just wasn't feeling well and was grumpy, and moody. Then I got some weird skin thing, and it turned out to be scabies. What the heck?! This is when things started to really go downhill. I had to coat myself from neck to toe in permethrin—a pesticide! We were heading to Australia for Christmas, and I had to fly on an airplane with this healing itchy rash all over my body. When we got back from our trip, I started to have these horrible experiences at night, where I'd wake up feeling like I was falling into oblivion. I was having panic attacks in my sleep. Simon was a certified therapist by now and calmed me down as much as he could.

I took two separate trips to the ER, convinced I was having a heart attack, which turned out to be panic attacks and anxiety. Everything checked out okay, but the ER doctor said I should get my thyroid checked. The next doctor ran a bunch of tests. One thing I haven't mentioned is that, for some reason in my life, I thought I was super cool if I didn't take any meds. I would wait until my migraine was full-blown, and I was nauseous before taking ibuprofen. I was barely eating, and I was exhausted. I was a forty-year-old woman, and all I wanted was my mom. I called in sick, curled up in a ball, and called my parents. They were here for two weeks. My mom cooked for me, took me to see an endocrinologist and cardiologist, and literally nursed me back to health. I had practically zero vitamin D, which turns out is a vital hormone. In addition, I had hypothyroidism and Hashimoto's—an autoimmune disease. Let me tell you, I was in the doldrums. Being diagnosed with so many things at one time was exhausting, especially since I wanted to understand every single detail. I was hesitant to be on so much medication, but I was desperate to feel better.

A great friend of ours who is a psychiatrist did an assessment and diagnosed me with anxiety and prescribed Lexapro. Looking back on various challenges in my life, I realized I had probably been dealing with anxiety for years. He saved my life by giving me the best advice that I will never forget. He said, "Don't suffer." He referred me to an amazing hypnotherapist, Anita Jung, who I saw for about a year. When your body is not absorbing vitamins and minerals, your mental state is affected. I had a nervous breakdown, literally taking one day at a time. Getting up out of bed, taking a shower, and getting dressed—each step was a huge and exhausting process. I spent a lot of time journaling, convincing myself everything was going to be okay.

Healing took time. Step by step, my vitamin D levels increased, my thyroid stabilized, I was eating healthy, going to yoga, taking my anxiety medication, journaling, and reconnecting with myself. Above all, I was learning how to slow down. Simon and I had some things to work on—who doesn't when one partner is going through a rough time? We learned a lot about each other and grew closer. I colored in coloring books and stared out the window, watching the birds. I listened to a lot of music. One weekend visiting my parents in Laredo, I met Fluffy, my fur-baby who is a four-pound

Chihuahua and Yorkshire terrier mix AKA Chorkie. Slowly, things started falling into place.

As a recovering overachiever, it's probably no surprise I did a ton of research on my own, but in this case, rather than burning me out, I learned how to heal. Every step I took and every new thing I learned has helped me in some way. I've also become very in-tune with and aware of my body. I've learned to truly listen to my gut, and this works for me. Ultimately, I've landed on an "everything in moderation" approach to food. Plus, you know—not as much sugar and ultra-processed foods.

After my burnout episode, I returned to work part-time in the corporate world, but once I was feeling strong enough, and I was back on my feet, I decided it was time to be my own boss.

I no longer wanted to sit within four walls in a cubicle commuting back and forth from home to the office. And this was pre-Covid! I wanted more control of my time and my schedule and to be paid what I was worth. I also wanted to focus on specializing in one thing that I really enjoyed and was really great at…Salesforce. I was tired of splitting my brain into ten different projects at a time. As much as I loved being a leader, I was tired of being everyone's counselor. I took a deep breath and quit my job (again). That master's degree sure came in handy working with people at all levels of an organization and becoming an influential leader.

After a few weeks, I called up one of my trusted mentors and told him my plan. He had started his own digital agency focused on marketing automation nine years prior. I said—I only want to work about twenty hours per week on Salesforce. If you have any clients that need support, I can subcontract for you. He was open to trying it out—so we signed the paperwork and away we went!

After a few months, I reached my twenty-hour-per-week goal. I loved it! Each day was different; I was working from home on my own schedule and making more money than I did working in a full-time corporate role. I could work on house projects, spend quality time with Simon, and exercise at barre3, which I loved. I also started family monthly potluck dinners. It was so fun bringing everyone together. Then, of course, Covid hit. This time, I really was in the right place at the right time. At first, I was unsure of the impact Covid would have on my job. I was already used to working from home. And companies still needed my Salesforce expertise. The work did not slow down. Fast forward eighteen months and I was up to forty hours per week again (some weeks even more!). But I was still loving it and really felt like I was adding value to our clients. Plus the income wasn't so bad either.

I soon realized the huge demand for Salesforce expertise and consulting and decided to recruit one of my best friends who had another full-time job. She wasn't happy in her role and it was 100% commission based. Knowing I was struggling with what to do next, she said she'd love to work with me. She worked with Salesforce daily in her current role so this would be a win-win for both of us. This was an eye-opener for me. I wanted to support other supersmart, experienced women who were mothers and couldn't work a full-time job, wanted flexibility, or wanted extra money. I started reaching out to women in my network who I had worked with previously and had always thought, "I'd love to work with her again someday." Looking back I realize now that I must have had a feeling I'd go down the road of becoming a business owner. Because I always earmarked these special women who I loved working with, knowing somehow our paths would cross again.

I formed an LLC and acquired a few direct clients. Eventually, I increased my rates and my clients didn't even bat an eye. We were an extension of their team, and we were providing tremendous value. I now have five amazing women working on my team. Some are full-time, and others are part-time. We have a handful of clients that contract us for anywhere between ten hours a month to twenty hours per week. The best part is that I get to run the business the way I want to. We are a very tight-knit group. We tell each other, "I love you," at the end of every other call. We laugh, we share challenges, and we troubleshoot complex business challenges together. Ultimately, they are my family.

While I was visiting family in New Zealand over the holidays, my father-in-law died of a heart attack. I had planned to be on vacation during this time but thought after the New Year I would check in with clients and do some work overlooking the beautiful landscape. I had to completely disconnect from work to plan the burial and be there for my husband and family. My team was amazing, and I didn't have to worry about anything. It made me realize I had built such an amazing group of leaders, partners, and friends that I could count on. My company continues growing steadily. I plan to grow the team and transition them to being W-2 employees, providing health benefits, and continuing to pay a top rate so everyone can have the opportunity to live their best life and achieve their goals and dreams.

However, I don't want to grow my business too fast or too big. My commitment to myself is to not lose myself in the overachieving swirl of always having to do more and make more money. I want to keep a balance and maintain the perspective of being able to have personable relationships with my team and clients.

After all, we are all human beings, trying to get through each day. We all attend conference calls with a million things going through our heads. As we get older, we worry about aging parents, kids in college, friends, and family members who are sick or just need a shoulder to cry on. It's all part of life. We have to preserve space for these moments and maintain self-care to be there for others when they need us. It's okay to take naps in the afternoon and stare out of the window, thinking about nothing. It's okay to sleep in on the weekends and not exercise every single day. These are all the things I've learned so far in my life, and I'm not even halfway there! Hi, I'm Janene—I'm a recovering overachiever.

JANENE NIBLOCK

Janene is the founder and chief SFDC Xpert of a woman-owned Salesforce consulting company, SFDC Xperts. With over eighteen years of operational business experience and superior knowledge of enterprise business systems, she leads a team of Salesforce experts and partners with organizations that require process automation and efficiency to accelerate growth and productivity within their workforce.

Janene lives in Austin, Texas, with her husband Simon and fur-baby Fluffy—a four-pound Chorkie and the love of her life (after her hubby, of course!). During her self-care time, she loves spending time with her hubby, sitting on the couch watching rom-coms, working on household projects, gardening, or baking sourdough bread. She also enjoys barre3, reading, listening to music with lyrics, and birdwatching. Coming from a big Hispanic family and being the oldest of seven, she enjoys getting the family together for gatherings!

https://www.linkedin.com/in/janeneniblock

12
PROMPTINGS OF THE HEART

SYLVIA WORSHAM

I n July 2008, as Hurricane Dolly tore a hole in the roof and water penetrated our home, my husband of nearly ten years asked for a divorce. Our young son, only four at the time, played quietly in the next room. Despite feeling like I couldn't breathe, deep down inside, relief washed over me like a cool breeze on a hot summer's day.

At twenty-four years of age, I married him, despite the gnawing in my gut telling me no. Many people thought it was the most beautiful ceremony they'd ever seen. However, I couldn't see the beauty in me. Years of bullying in high school did their job of crushing any confidence I had left. I didn't believe I was beautiful enough to receive a marriage proposal from anyone else, so I said yes to him. I thought he was my only option. As I gripped my father's arm tightly, my chest felt tight, and the walls of the church closed in on me as we slowly made our way down the altar to the man I would soon call, "my husband."

From the outside, our lives looked picture-perfect—the corporate wife, the business-owner husband, and a happy son—the ideal family living in a prominent neighborhood. We attended Catholic church every Sunday. We checked off all the boxes that society expected us to achieve. He knew how to put on a show—portraying himself as this loving husband to the churchgoers, but as soon as we got home, he would retreat to watch football. I pretended my life fulfilled me, but at the core, I didn't feel happy. For years, a war raged between my mind and my heart to leave him. Despite feeling this way, the perfectionist and security seeker in me prolonged my stay in this loveless marriage.

After our divorce, our family therapist recommended that we keep our son in the same home and school to meet his security needs. My responsibility was to provide $2,000 for the mortgage and private school tuition. His father refused to pay for additional expenses beyond what was deemed necessary. Divorce reinforced my belief of "I am not enough" and kicked my guilt into high gear. I began working long hours to meet my financial obligations and to avoid these feelings of shame.

A few months prior to my divorce, my company, Pfizer, had promoted me to a higher-level position. This was after four years of rejections. I had applied for various upper-level positions, only to be told "no." The senior vice president and regional manager held insurmountable expectations to turn around my underperforming hospital sales territory that was second to last in a region within six months of my placement.

My soul felt the pull to use change as the catalyst to gain a deeper awareness of my faith in God. Even though I grew up attending Catholic schools, I didn't have a relationship with Him. I felt a disconnect from religion after my divorce since they frowned on it. In all my years as a Catholic, I never knew how to talk or pray to God.

I wrote daily in my journal to declutter my mind and to hear God's voice. The consistency of this practice allowed me to gain a deeper awareness of my inner guidance, instead of looking for my answers in my achievements, relationships, career, or religion. As change roared at me in my personal and professional life, God placed a desire in my heart to become number one in my sales division.

My fear of the unknown kept me obsessing and stressing about my future. As any single mom understands, my greatest concern focused solely on my little boy. "How will his father's absence affect him?" "Will I be able to provide financially for his needs?"

In April 2009, nine months after my husband asked for a divorce, 300 of my Pfizer peers listened intently to me as I stood on stage and recounted how my sales territory landed in the number one spot in the region. My heart pounded loudly inside my chest, and the spotlight shined brightly above me. It was one of the most rewarding experiences of my life, and, yet, I felt guilty and ashamed for the long hours I'd put in. Somewhere deep inside of me, a thought formed: I, too, had abandoned my boy in his hour of need.

In retrospect, it's evident how my subconscious programming (my old ego identity) played a role in downplaying my joy and sense of fulfillment. My Mexican and Catholic upbringing taught me that a woman could not have it all without sacrificing something. This belief was not mine but became my truth and compounded the more I thought and acted on it.

As I journeyed through this difficult period in my life, I found God's love for me was immense and pure. He saw my needs and desires and offered me opportunities to enjoy. But, unfortunately, my emotional mind stopped me from feeling joy. Instead, it relied on the negative beliefs, thoughts, feelings, habits, and patterns I fed it consistently.

When I learned to love myself as He loved me, I saw myself as He saw me—whole, gifted, and worthy of joy and fulfillment. I began to take care of myself mentally, physically, emotionally, and spiritually, which benefited my overall sense of well-being. I began to praise myself for goals achieved instead of striving for more because I couldn't "see" my worth. It freed me from the fear, guilt, and shame holding me back from confidently stepping into change.

I was unaware of my subconscious choice to carry feelings of guilt and shame for events entirely out of my control. It wreaked havoc on my relationships. Catastrophically, it impacted my bond with my son. I subconsciously projected the heavy burden I felt inside on my young boy, which his mind picked up on. Unfortunately, it became part of his belief system, too. He associated long hours at work with abandonment, which resulted in self-sabotage. His mind rejected being an achiever. Today, he's actively working with a coach to reframe this belief.

Being an achiever is not a bad thing. However, if the motivation behind it is informed by fearful beliefs and feelings, it will rob you of joy and happiness. More than once, I've thought, "Once I get there, I will be happy." Don't worry, plenty of people, including myself, have believed this to be true. After many years of allowing this belief to steer my choices, the realization finally hit me like a ton of bricks —getting "there" is an illusion your emotional mind makes to give you certainty. As Ralph Waldo Emerson brilliantly wrote, "Life is a journey, not a destination."

I learned that joy lives within me because God resides inside. When I stay in the present moment and operate from love and gratitude, I will find Him. Nothing outside of me will bring me the happiness I seek, because I create and give myself that happiness. The biggest lesson I learned was that joy and happiness have been there all along, hidden below my fear.

What I needed was a big dose of grace, which I, unfortunately, didn't give myself as I traveled from fear to joy. Now, I know I did the best job I could at the time, and over time, I forgave myself and released this guilt and shame to God.

In my first book, *Journey to Me: Trust the Wisdom of Change*, I shared a visualization technique I learned long ago. Picture yourself standing in the middle of a tornado, and imagine your negative feelings being ripped out of you. Stand firmly, grounded in your power, and allow the feelings to move through you and upward toward the sky where Gods' hands are outstretched, ready to receive them from you. Do this exercise consistently until you feel the negative feelings are gone from your spirit. Since I was a stubborn child of God, intent on "overthinking my way through life," it took me months of consistent practice to diminish their power over me.

Three years after the divorce, and at a turning point, God whispered, "You need to go" to a party my college friend had invited me to months before. During this time, my consistent prayers to God were to help me find "the one." Despite receiving the devastating news from my employer, Pfizer, that they planned layoffs in our division, this persistent thought dominated my mind for a week or so. Finally, I followed my heart's prompting and drove six hours to Houston, Texas. Not knowing anyone there aside from my friend's family did not deter me from mingling with 200 of her friends, and I met Donnie.

We began a long-distance relationship, seeing each other every two weeks on the weekends my son spent with his dad. My face radiated love and happiness whenever anyone mentioned his name. Within four months of dating, Donnie invited my son to meet his family in Louisiana on Easter Weekend in 2012. For a single mom, it was a sure sign he intended to marry me. Three days before departure, a pain developed in my chest. I intended to take our flight to Houston on our way to Louisiana regardless of my body's obvious physical signs of distress.

After a night of excruciating pain, which felt like fifty knives piercing my chest, I walked into the emergency room of St. Luke's Episcopal Hospital unassisted, and their team promptly escorted me toward the back.

After a series of scans on my lungs, a specialist walked into my ER holding room and boldly stated, "A woman in your condition should not be talking to me right now." He was shocked and bewildered. Two blood clots the size of dimes traveled through my heart and failed to stop it. He explained to me that in order for them to get to my lungs, they made their way through the veins in my heart, which in most cases prove fatal. As frightening as this encounter was, it paled in comparison to what happened next.

A group of six doctors, "the firing squad," as I often refer to them in interviews, entered my hospital room Saturday afternoon of Easter weekend to share what a second scan of my abdomen showed. From my vantage point, I noticed they avoided eye contact with me. The rapid fire of words came at me like bullets: liver transplant, stroke, and death. Just as the terms reached me, a numbing feeling encircled me.

In a moment of terror and disbelief, my eyes closed as I visualized falling into God's loving arms in complete and total surrender. I trusted and believed He would provide me with a second chance at life. But, unbeknownst to me, they had shared my prognosis with my family, "She has a 20% chance of survival."

The next morning, on Easter Sunday, a woman with the Catholic Diocese entered my intensive care unit room and asked if she could pray with me. She, Donnie, and I formed a circle and began reciting the Our Father when, suddenly, a love enveloped the whole room. God cradled my broken spirit and assured me He heard my prayers. Peace washed over my entire being. When she left, Donnie turned to me and said, "You felt Him too, didn't you?" With tears of joy in my eyes, I managed to mumble, "Yes."

God granted me three miracles within seventy-two hours during Easter weekend in 2012, which profoundly impacted my health, mindset, relationships, and career. The first miracle occurred when God prompted me, "Lean forward, and you'll be able to breathe," the night the two blood clots traveled through the veins of my heart, saving me from dying in the middle of the night. The second miracle occurred when God's love assured me that He heard my prayers and granted me a second chance. The final miracle God gifted me was survival without long-term effects, something that shocked the doctors who deemed it impossible!

This near-death experience awakened me to the value of surrender and deepened my connection to God. It helped me transition from believing in Him to trusting Him implicitly, which guided me toward my divine soul's purpose.

> Trust in and rely confidently on the Lord with all your heart and do not rely on your own insight or understanding. In all your ways know and acknowledge and recognize Him. And He will make your paths straight and smooth.
>
> Proverbs 3: 5-6

Fear accompanied me for many years, blocking my joy and happiness. Those fear-driven choices kept me shackled to the pharmaceutical and medical device world longer than God wanted. It was a prime breeding ground for a perfectionist and high achiever who persistently strove to attain her desired happiness. The more I gave, the more the corporate world wanted from me. My relationship with Him deepened after my crisis, yet it would take time before my past ego released me to follow God's master plan.

My health turning point propelled me toward discovering why God granted me a second chance. Six months after nearly dying, I took the leap of faith, moved to Austin, with my young son, and married Donnie. Trading in my comfortable corporate job and beginning again in a different branch of medical sales brought a new awareness that God used to show me my next steps.

Donnie dreamed of having a biological child with me, so within a few months of meetings with multiple specialists to ensure a safe pregnancy, we decided to start our journey to expand our family. A short time later, we received the happy news. On my second doctor's visit, Donnie joined to meet his baby. We walked into our appointment with our hearts full and happy.

Within minutes of starting the sonogram, Dr. Phillips face changed from jovial to worried. He said, "Guys, I have bad news. I don't see a heartbeat. I'm so sorry." My eyes filled with tears as Donnie looked shocked. Dr. Phillips squeezed our hands and walked out to give us a moment to ourselves. We held each other and sobbed. To add to the trauma, Dr. Phillips told us he needed to perform a procedure to take our baby out. With heavy hearts and broken dreams, we walked out slowly with our shoulders drooped. The stress of being on my feet twelve hours a day and answering to belligerent doctors in medical device sales likely caused my miscarriage.

My grief became my constant companion for the next six weeks, and I retired from medical sales the morning of the devastating news from Dr. Phillips. Donnie walked around like a zombie engrossed in his work. My days were long and silent with only my anxious thoughts to keep me company.

In April 2014, two months after our miscarriage, we found out that we were expecting another baby. Taking time off without a plan seemed nerve-wracking for the doer in me, but I learned to trust God's voice. Slowing down helped me focus on other areas of my life that lacked the fulfillment I sought. Yet, the struggle became real pretty quickly after that. It was a rude awakening to transition from a six-thirty a.m. to ten-thirty p.m. stressed-out achiever to a stay-at-home parent. The hardest lesson in my consciousness was, **"Be patient with God's timing."**

If you are anything like me, patience is NOT your strong suit. In profound conversations with my Heavenly Father, it became evident, He intended to use the time to chisel away unwanted belief systems to allow the light inside me to shine brightly. Instead of leaning into this change, my ego resisted it.

To live in the NOW took enormous focus. Such as Julia Roberts portrayed in the movie, *Eat, Pray, Love* when she sat there intently trying to pray only to discover time traveled slower when you weren't busy ignoring the pain inside you. Like Julia, meditating and sitting still for even a few minutes felt like an eternity for me, who experienced a smorgasbord of thoughts and the itch to move. However, the more I did it, the easier it got.

Daily, I journaled three pages to hear God's voice above the outside world's noise. I took personal development courses, read John

Maxwell books, and actively looked for God in my everyday life. Then one day, as my baby girl busily rocked back and forth on her baby swing, another prompting pushed its way to the forefront, "Call Bridget."

Years before in 2011, I took a twelve-week John Maxwell Mastermind that Bridget led. Soon afterward, she invited me to become part of the John Maxwell team as a speaker, coach, and trainer. But my old identity, which rooted itself in certainty, put that dream on hold.

Bridget answered on the second ring, she picked up, and proceeded to direct me toward the certification team. After speaking with Donnie, I took the plunge into the coaching and speaking industry. God continued to lead me with every prompting He placed in my heart. Turning inward revealed my next step.

In August 2017, my dream to become a speaker, coach, and trainer with the John Maxwell team was realized. God sent me ample opportunities to build my business, one sector at a time, all in divine timing. Just as my career bloomed, my home life unraveled. My family felt they weren't enough for me: notably my husband and son. Their own subconscious programming and patterns reared their ugly heads as a change in our home atmosphere heightened with my new role. Over time and several conversations later, Donnie understood the "pull" I felt to step into God's master plan for my life and supported my move wholeheartedly. I lovingly addressed my new role with my son and explained to him, "Mom is a different person today, sweetheart. She understands the importance of balancing her home life with her career."

As this new stage in my development threatened to derail our family unity, two identities emerged within me. An epic battle ensued. On the one hand, my old ego identity promoted guilt and shame at stepping into this new role. It likely stemmed from old belief systems of feeling that I had abandoned my son for work after the divorce. Then, my soul identity encouraged me to propel toward my divine soul's purpose of guiding women from turning points to breakthroughs. These feelings persisted until March 2020, as the pandemic erupted, when suddenly, everything became clear.

An insistent thought and prompting from God broke through loud and clear, "Write your book, trust me, it's time." A transformation took shape within me with every stroke of the pen. By reflecting on my past experiences and God's role in each chapter, I soon uncovered what He intended for me to see. When I acted on His guidance, He came through abundantly for me. The realization suddenly hit me, "Life is meant to be journeyed joyfully with God by your side."

He created me to be free from fear and to find joy in the journey. He showed me the gifts He had given me since my birth, and I developed them one by one as time passed. My confidence, faith, and joy soared after becoming an author in October 2021 with the publication of *Journey to Me: Trust the Wisdom of Change* and the subsequent publications in other collaborative works.

> I am the vine, you are the branches. He who abides in Me, and I
> in turn, bears much fruit; for without Me, you can do nothing.

John 15:5

We operated as one unit while writing my first book, and this experience led me to continue this as my new normal. My subconscious programming, old fear-based beliefs, and traumas ceased to dictate my choices in life. Additionally, God would lead the way, and I, His faithful servant, joyfully followed.

Each turning point showed me God's hand in my life. What He taught me through the wisdom of change was that when I lovingly surrendered to the promptings of my heart and acted on His timing, He led me out of my fear and ego and toward my soul's desires where joy and fulfillment patiently waited for me. My transformation took me from a perfectionist who felt insignificant unless she achieved something to a worthy and gifted author, speaker, and coach who knows her value and boldly lives her passion daily.

When I reflect today, I see Jesus' footprints in my journey. He was there all along, whispering His words of encouragement, love, and belief to me in the promptings my heart received. I see and find joy in my everyday life. It's present in an early morning snuggle with my young daughter, an impromptu duet with my son in the car, and a lingering and loving gaze from my husband. To arrive at this point in my life took a bold vision that stretched me beyond my comfort zone, trusting God by acting on His guidance, and a consistent daily effort to follow my purpose with passion, despite the roadblocks. Since the advent of this amazing discovery, I rely on His promptings to enlighten my path.

The more I surrender control daily to God, allow the flow of life, release the feelings, beliefs, and old programming to my Heavenly Father, choose to operate from a space of love and joy instead of fear, and act on the promptings of my heart, I feel fulfillment. This in turn attracts ample opportunities to apply my God-given gifts to humanity as He intended me to do. It feels thrilling to live in the NOW, free from fear, with curiosity and anticipation to see what God has in store for my beautiful life!

SYLVIA WORSHAM

Sylvia Worsham received three miracles in seventy-two hours during Easter weekend in 2012. She traded her multiple award-winning sales careers at Pfizer & Roche to become the international best-selling author, multilingual speaker, and Turning Points Coach she is today.

Sylvia lives her passion by helping corporate and professional women who are in deep spiritual change to navigate toward their divine soul's purpose and align with their soul's identity. She does this through her writing, podcast interviews, Joy in the Journey masterminds, keynote addresses, and one-on-one coaching. She resides in Austin, Texas, with her amazing husband, two children, and dog.

https://www.linkedin.com/in/sylviaworsham/
https://www.facebook.com/coachsylviaworsham
https://www.instagram.com/coachsylviaworsham/

13

SPACEY STACY

STACY JOHNSON

The nickname Spacey Stacy wasn't bestowed upon me in third grade for nothing. There was no specific event that prompted the nickname; I suppose it was just my everyday behavior. Little did I know, my silly moniker may well have been one of the early signs of my neurodivergence, ADHD. Severe ADHD. Interestingly, I consider ADHD my superpower, but also my greatest weakness.

Today, I know that I'm wildly successful. But as I write this sentence, I'm immediately filled with unease because I don't often feel like a success, and self-doubt is something I've struggled with my whole life. Low self-esteem, imposter syndrome, feeling less-than...these are feelings I blamed on my childhood trauma and repetitive abandonment by foster families as a tween and teen, but now I know there's another culprit. ADHD comes with a little-known symptom called RSD, or rejection sensitivity dysphoria.

If you could hear the thoughts that run through my head on a regular basis, you would NEVER believe that I'm living my dream as the founder and CEO of an award-winning nonprofit organization for foster children called Central Texas Table of Grace. Or that I have received a miraculous level of support from my community since the day I started this journey over eight years ago. Or that I have been nominated for and received more awards than I can remember or name, including the True Inspiration Award, the Champion for Children Award, the Austin Icon for Children Award, the Service to Mankind Award, the Young Leader Award, and the NBC/KXAN Most Remarkable Woman in Texas.

If you could eavesdrop on my thoughts, you might not gather that I have an incredible husband, family, and home life. And a new puppy named Jack. From the outside looking in, most would say I have it all. From the feedback I get, I apparently make it look effortless. As if all my dreams came true overnight. I think the very reason I decided to participate in this book is that this couldn't be further from the truth. However, I noticed that's how I tend to view the success of others too. That's why it was so important for me to share how messy it can feel and look in the thick of it. I think most of us compare ourselves to others. It shouldn't be done, but if we're going to do it anyway, wouldn't it be helpful to know the *real* story, what it *really* took, and how it *really* felt?

Despite some early difficulty in school with paying attention, hence my childhood nickname, my ADHD symptoms became more noticeable in my twenties. I got hired at COUNTRY Financial as an insurance agent and financial advisor a few years after I moved to Bend, Oregon, to be closer to some of my biological family members. Despite learning quickly and consistently smashing sales goals, I began to see a pattern. Evidently, my messy desk, my chaotic personal life (that I often over-shared), my disorganization, my impulsivity, and my forgetfulness invited the judgment of others. The comments often made me feel like I was being viewed as an irresponsible, unintelligent, flighty blonde. Coworkers, supervisors, and even friends made comments. My work bestie would look at me often, shake her head, and say, "Sometimes I wonder how you make it through the day...." I can still remember some of the cringy things I said because of the inability to think before I spoke that surely made me appear like the least intelligent person on earth. Remember some of Jessica Simpson's ditziest comments that everyone still talks about? "No thank you, I don't eat buffalo," when offered a buffalo wing. I've said things like that.

After a very successful eight years at COUNTRY Financial, I decided to move to Austin. COUNTRY Financial wasn't in the state of Texas, so I could not transfer. I quickly realized that most firms required a college degree as a prerequisite, and a degree was something I did not possess. Despite growing up in California where college for foster kids is subsidized, I lacked the guidance to navigate that path and jumped right into working.

My childhood was traumatic and unpredictable. I had gone through ten foster homes before being moved to a group home when I was fifteen. I told the group home therapist that I wanted to be legally emancipated and on my own by the time I was sixteen. Instead of brushing off my hope or my goal, he saw me not for who I was, but for who I could be. He believed in me and told me I could do it. I got a job at a convalescent hospital as a nursing assistant, and after three months became certified by the state as a CNA. On Cinco de Mayo, at the age of sixteen, I was legally emancipated by the judge and officially on my own. I lived in my own apartment and graduated high school while working full-time.

I thought I was going to go on to become an RN but quickly realized my squeamishness wouldn't allow that. A little over a year later, I got a job at Kinko's, the copy store. I moved up through the ranks, eventually making it to major account manager, where I wore a suit to work and had professional responsibilities, but was still making less than ten dollars an hour. I knew I needed to get a second job; I wasn't able to stay afloat with my income. When I was offered an interview at COUNTRY Financial, my whole life changed. I got the job right before my twenty-first birthday, and in my first year, I made more money than I ever could've dreamed of. I never thought about going to college. When I was faced with having to pivot at age twenty-nine to a new career in Texas as a single mom, I remember being told by a close friend that I should try the car business since selling cars doesn't require a degree. He told me if I was good at it and worked hard, I could make six figures easily.

Sounded good to me! I sold everything I owned and flew to Texas with my seven-month-old daughter. Two car dealerships offered me a job. I took the second one at Ford, and sure enough, my financial needs were more than met! Life in Texas was working out well!

Reflecting on the day I got emancipated at age sixteen, I remember thinking that someday I was going to help foster kids the way Russ at the group home had helped me. Maybe I'd open my own group home one day. Of course, being on my own at sixteen wasn't very easy, and when I got the job at COUNTRY Financial, I imagined that would be my career for life. After all, I liked it, and I was good at it. I made great money, had a corner office overlooking the river, loved my colleagues and co-workers, and won trips and awards every single year. I'm not sure I thought much about my dream of helping foster kids beyond that day in court. I really couldn't tell you why I brought it up on my second date with Bill thirteen years later, but that's what I did.

"If that's your dream, you should just do it," he said. I looked at him as if he had just informed me he was from planet Mars.

"I'm a single mom making good money; I can't just quit my job and start a nonprofit, but thanks for the encouragement," I responded. I may or may not have rolled my eyes. But when he walked me to my car, he said it again. I brushed him off a second time and made a mental note not to bring it up again *if* we had another date. Later that night, he texted me that I should check my email. Would you believe he sent me an e-book called *Sarah Johnson's Guide to Opening a Group Home?* By the next morning, I had read the entire book, and I was on step five. From that day forward, there was an invisible force (I think it's called passion) pushing me to take the steps. I kept taking the steps and taking the steps while grinding away at Maxwell Ford.

Around the same time, I noticed that despite being in this new city, with my new job and new coworkers at the dealership, it appeared I was still being perceived in the same way. ADHD was now somewhat of a buzzword, so instead of calling me a space cadet or asking me how I make it through the day, I would hear things like,

"Gosh you're so ADHD," "It's ok, all salespeople are ADHD," and "Time to take your medication." It was starting to bother me. I had an amazing business coach in my twenties that had impressed upon me how much thoughts and words matter. I didn't want these assessments of my mental health to be a self-fulfilling prophecy or cause me any more shame, so I decided to pursue a diagnosis. Either I have it or I don't. Either these are deep-seated personality traits, nasty habits I need to break, or signs of a treatable mental health issue. I would decide for myself if these things were affecting my life, but until I knew what these things were and why I was the way I was, there was nothing I could do. I needed more information.

We all know there's a stigma around mental health. Maybe that's why it took me a few more *years* to make the appointment. By this time, I had realized my dream of opening a group home. When I arrived for my appointment at Central Texas Mental Health, I checked in and was handed an iPad. The electronic questionnaire was an assessment looking for signs of five disorders—ADHD, OCD, bipolar, depression, and anxiety. After completing the test and waiting some more, I was finally called back, and I spoke with the psychiatrist for about fifteen minutes. I suppose I've already spoiled the surprise...my diagnosis was severe ADHD. He wrote me a prescription for a low dose of Adderall and sent me on my way. I really struggled with whether or not to take the medication. Addiction runs in my family. The research I was doing wasn't giving me a clear feeling of YES or NO, and I worried that maybe the medication would change me or my personality. Maybe I wouldn't be me anymore? Did I even want to be me anymore? A few months later, something made up my mind for me.

At the ripe old age of thirty-five, I enrolled in college. I had been running my group home for a few years when I noticed a major risk exposure in my organization. As a residential childcare operator, I am required to have a licensed childcare administrator on staff at all times. This is a special state certification. However, the prerequisite is a college degree. Licensed childcare administrators make a very high salary at larger organizations, which put me in a tough spot.

Our meager budget would not support that kind of wage, and in addition, LCCAs are difficult to find. They have to have a college degree, pass the state test, AND have multiple years of experience in a *residential* operation—so it couldn't be someone fresh out of college, a teacher, or a daycare worker—they have to have multiple years of experience in a facility where children LIVE. The pickings are slim, and it really hit home when my LCCA moved and I had difficulty finding another one. Luckily, I found someone at the last minute before The Department of Family and Protective Services pulled my kids, which was just days away from happening. I knew then that I would need to become the backup LCCA. I enrolled in school full-time while continuing to work full-time leading my organization. A week later, I started the medication.

As leaders, we are expected to be poised and polished and always have it together. Unfortunately, the phrases that might describe someone showing ADHD traits don't describe a great leader: procrastinator, unorganized, always late, easily distracted, impulsive, forgetful, inconsistent, lazy. Some symptoms of ADHD can cause quite serious issues. According to the Diagnostic and Statistical Manual of Mental Disorders, ADHD is diagnosed in adults when five or more symptoms of inattention and/or hyperactivity have been present for at least six months, in addition to a few other qualifiers. I have nine out of nine. My diagnosis is "combined presentation," which means I have both inattentive and hyperactivity, or impulsivity, traits. When ADHD traits are on full display in life, serious consequences can occur. For instance, forgetfulness can cause a failure to appear for something simple like a traffic ticket. Impulsivity can cause spending that results in massive debt or risk-taking with drugs, alcohol, or sex (sometimes all three). Addiction is very common in ADHDers.

As leaders, how can we get support when we're so worried about our imperfections showing? Maybe if I had known that those whom I admire have mental health struggles too, I would have taken care of myself sooner. If this helps ONE person decide to get help, I'm happy to let my imperfections be known. I remember agonizing over the medication decision. Looking back now, I know I never would've graduated college without it. Believe it or not, I graduated magna cum laude with my bachelor's in public administration in less than four years while working full-time. You see, ADHD is a paradoxical condition. ADHDers have difficulty focusing combined with an innate ability to super focus, procrastination tendencies combined with the ability to get a full day's worth of work done within an hour, impulsive and foolish decision-making combined with incredible innovation and problem-solving skills, interpersonal obliviousness combined with intuitive and empathic traits. For every negative ADHD trait, there is a positive one. My ADHD allows me to hyperfocus on things that are important to me; I'm an absolute visionary when it comes to my passion for foster care. I have a lightning-quick mind. I perform best under pressure and thrive in highly stimulating situations.

Putting myself first and focusing on my mental health is imperative as a leader. All of the things I avoided doing to help myself because of how they might make me appear are the very things that allowed me to turn my greatest weakness into my superpower. I've learned so much throughout my mental health struggles. Not only about ADHD but about life in general. There are some skills and habits I've adopted that serve me well. My first step in the midst of any struggle or adversity is always to get more information. Any problem or issue I encounter can usually be solved more easily when I have more information. All the research I have done and continue to do regarding ADHD equips me to embrace my neurological tendencies and do things in the ways that work best for me. Would you believe I've learned more about ADHD and how to manage it from TikTok than from any psychiatrist or psychologist? I always verify the information (we can't believe everything we see online), but the platform has opened my eyes to many aspects of the disorder and what it means to me. It also shows me I'm not alone in this struggle, and I'm able to try things that have helped others. Connecting with those who have similar experiences can be very helpful.

165

At first, I was too embarrassed to talk to anyone in my life about my mental health. As I mentioned earlier, rejection sensitive dysphoria (RSD) is a major symptom of ADHD. RSD is the experience of severe emotional pain because of failure or feeling rejected. This isn't just the normal rumination we all feel after a negative interaction; this is a severe presentation of emotional outbursts or sadness because of criticism or rejection (real or perceived). Now that I know about RSD, there are things I can do to mitigate it and respond appropriately, despite my thoughts or feelings. Another life-changer for me was finding an ADHD coach. Yes, that's a thing. I've always had great results with life coaches and business coaches, so when my husband found an ADHD coach, I was all in! She has given me so much insight and keeps me on track week to week. She also taught me to be kind to myself and to have grace and compassion for myself when I have a tough day.

Our mental health disorders and differences are not our fault, but they are our responsibility to manage. There is beauty in imperfection, being a work in progress. Stay in the game, take it a day at a time. The greatest joy isn't in achieving success and the perfect outcome, the joy is in the game itself. The joy is in figuring it out, taking the leaps, and doing the work. The good news is that the information is always out there. And when you find it, pay it forward —don't forget to show your work!

STACY JOHNSON

After leaving an alcoholic and neglectful mother and entering the foster care system at the age of two, Stacy Johnson spent the next fourteen years moving from foster home to foster home, dreaming that someday she would open a children's shelter and help other kids like herself. In May 2014, that dream came to fruition as she finally opened the doors of Central Texas Table of Grace, a 501(c)(3) nonprofit organization that exists to provide emergency shelter services to foster children and administers a Supervised Independent Living program for young adults aging out of foster care.

In 2021, NBC's KXAN recognized Stacy as the "Most Remarkable Woman of the Year" in Central Texas. In 2022, the Texas Women's Foundation selected Stacy for their "Young Leader Award," and she was featured by Success Magazine in their inaugural Women of Influence issue.

https://www.facebook.com/stacyjoleighjohnson/
https://www.instagram.com/stacyjoleighjohnson/
https://www.linkedin.com/in/stacyjohnsoncttg/
https://www.tiktok.com/@stacyjoleigh

CHILDREN'S EMERGENCY SHELTER

All proceeds from this multi-author book are donated to Central Texas Table of Grace.

Central Texas Table of Grace is a 501(c)(3) non-profit organization that exists to provide emergency shelter services to the foster children and administers Grace365 Supervised Independent Living program for young adults aging out of foster care. Their support contributes to an improved quality of life for youth and their families. The organization's projects, implemented by an experienced staff, emphasize creating a caring climate for youth. Supporting the development of self-confidence, healthful living, and good judgment, Central Texas Table of Grace provides our children with a thorough foundation for success.

Follow Central Texas Table of Grace on social media to find out more.
https://www.facebook.com/centraltexastableofgrace
https://www.instagram.com/ctxtableofgrace/
https://www.linkedin.com/company/central-texas-table-of-grace/
https://twitter.com/CTXTableOfGrace
https://www.tiktok.com/@ctxtableofgrace

ABOUT SULIT PRESS

S ulit Press is a boutique publishing house that provides high-touch support to thought leaders, industry shakers, and changemakers writing impactful nonfiction books. Whether you're interested in publishing your **personal memoir** or industry-specific **solo books,** or joining high-vibe, collaborative **multi-author books**, we'll help you transition from *aspiring* author to *published* author!

Founder and CEO Michelle Savage is an international best-selling author, editor, and author mentor. From her experience of walking authors through the publishing process with other publishing houses, Michelle discovered a gaping hole in the market—finding publishers who care enough about their authors to provide a cohesive publishing process and deliver on their promises. Sulit Press was born from Michelle's desire to create a boutique publishing space that offers personalized support through every step and invests deeply in the success of every single author.